19TH-CENTURY
RUSSIAN LITERATURE

-NINE GOLDEN VOICES-

DONALD E. BROWN

authorHOUSE®

AuthorHouse™
1663 Liberty Drive
Bloomington, IN 47403
www.authorhouse.com
Phone: 833-262-8899

Published by AuthorHouse 09/02/2022

ISBN: 978-1-6655-6902-6 (sc)
ISBN: 978-1-6655-6901-9 (e)

Library of Congress Control Number: 2022915585

Print information available on the last page.

CONTENTS

PREFACE

I was first introduced to nineteenth Russian literature when Mr. Sabo, my high school sophomore English teacher, had me read and openly discuss - in front of the class - my interpretation of several excerpts similar to this from Leo Tolstoy's "War and Peace": "When a man finds himself in motion he always devises some purpose for his bodily exertion. To be able to walk hundreds of miles a man must believe that something good awaits him at the end of those hundreds of miles. He needs the prospect of a promised land to give him the strength to keep on."

My knowledge of the literary works of writers from what is called "The Golden Age" of Russian literature, was further deepen in a two semester comparative literature course I took in college. Although many, many decades have passed since high school and college, my appreciation and understanding of the universality of Tolstoy, Chekhov, Goncharova, Pushkin, and other nineteenth century Russian writers have slowly seasoned as I've aged and matured.

There are three reason I enjoy the literary works of nineteenth century Russian writers and thinkers: First and foremost these writers were storytellers, spokesmen, agitators, and political symbols. Literature provided them one of the few platforms on which they could assess the country and state their views of the world. However, writing honestly during that time in Russia was risky; and the consequences included denouncement, harassment, imprisonment, censorship, exile, or execution. These writers were the conscience of their country and time. Second, the primary theme running through this "Golden Age" literature was social inequity. During this period the Russian lower class started to become more aware of the unjust treatment they received from those in positions of power. Russian writers began to addressed these issues in their works, thereby, giving rise to public discourse on serfdom and inequalities. And third, nineteenth century Russian literature was widely recognized for its ability to accurately capture human sentiment through fictitious characters. By detailing human experiences nineteenth century Russian writers—ranging from Pushkin to Garshin to Gorky —created works that have transcended time and left legacies that will extend and touch the souls of readers well into the future.

As you read the passages from various novels, short stories, letters, and essays written by nine of these great writers of nineteenth century Russian literature, I hope you, like me, will be inspired to discover, read, appreciate, and enjoy the beauty and sensitivity expressed in the written words of these amazing literary artists.

DEDICATION

I proudly dedicated this, my first published work, to my wonderful wife, Glennette Brown. Her support, understanding, and patience helped make this a reality. I also wish to dedicate this book to and thank three amazing human beings, my children Kobie Brown, Njeri Brown, and Nia Brown, who inspired, encouraged and cheered me on. I am forever grateful to my grandparents, father, mother, stepfather, brother, and namesake (Uncle Donald) whose sacrifices, wisdom, unconditional love and kindness provided the moral compass which allowed me to chart my journey through life. And last, I want to thank Mr. Sabo, my high school sophomore teacher, and the college comparative literature professors for providing the spark that ignited my life-long interest in a unique group of writers whose literary works belong to all humanity.

CHAPTER ONE

Ivan Aleksandrovich Goncharov (1812-91)

* *Recognized as a critical realist who presented ordinary surroundings and endeavors.*
* *Addressed injustices and dramatized social changes in Russia.*
* *A "cool and detached observer" who create powerful lifelike images.*
* *More interested in people as they are and less in trying to change them.*
* *Quoted as saying that the purpose of his novels, "is to present the eternal struggle between East and West."*
* *A shy and retiring individual with few intimate friends.*
* *Exhibited paranoid behavior which was first displayed during his teenage years.*

"Oblomov"

Ilya Oblomov epitomizes the early nineteenth century Russian serf-owning landed gentry. He is lazy, lacking in ambition, initiative and purpose. He is an alienated dreamer who cannot, or will not, adjust to a changing society. Instead of even searching for an alternative to a declining way of life, Oblomov often dreams, reminisces and remains committed to the ways of his childhood village of Oblomovka. Despite advice or support from a childhood friend, and the love of a caring woman, Oblomov continues to live in his world of apathetic fantasy. And finds refuge in the shabby lodging of a motherly widow that becomes a blissful surrogate for the village of Oblomovka.

Passages from "Oblomov"

"..a total absence of any definite idea,.."

"He was a man of about thirty-two or three, of medium height and pleasant appearance, with dark grey eyes, but with a total absence of any definite idea, any concentration, in his features. Thoughts promenaded freely all over his face, fluttered about in his eyes, reposed on his half-parted lips, conceded themselves in the furrows of his brow, and then vanished completely—and it was at such moments that an expression of serene unconcern spread all over his face. This unconcern passed from his face into the contours of his body and even into the folds of his dressing gown."

The narrator goes on to provide these additional descriptions and opinions:

"Occasionally a sombre look of something like fatigue or boredom crept into his eyes; but neither fatigue nor boredom could banish for a moment the mildness which was the predominant and fundamental expression not only on his face but of his whole soul, so serenely and unashamedly reflected in his eyes, his smile and every movement of his head and hands. A cold and superficial observer, casting a passing glance at Oblomov, would have said: "A good-natured fellow, I'll be bound, a simpleton!" A more thoughtful and sympathetic man, after a long scrutiny of his face, would have walked away with a smile, full of pleasant thoughts."

"..a chain of gently sloping hillocks,.."

"The sky there seems to hug the earth, not in order to fling its thunderbolts at it, but to embrace it more tightly and lovingly; it hangs as low overhead as the trustworthy roof of the parental house, to preserve, it would seem, the chosen spot from all calamities. The sun there shines brightly and warmly for about six months of the year and withdraws gradually, as though reluctantly, as though turning back to take another look at the place it loves and to give it a warm, clear day in the autumn, amid the rain and slush. The mountains there seem to be only small-scale models of the terrifying mountains far away that frighten the imagination. They form a chain of gently sloping hillocks, down which it is pleasant to slide on one's back in play, or to sit on watching the sunset dreamily."

"..an imperturbable stillness fell..."

"At midday it was hot; not a cloud in the sky. The sun stood motionless overhead scorching the grass. There was not the faintest breeze in the motionless air. Neither tree nor water stirred; an imperturbable stillness fell over the village and the fields, as though everything were dead. The human voice sounded loud and clear in the empty air. The flight and the buzzing of a beetle could be heard a hundred yards away, and from the thick grass there came the sound of snorting, as if someone was fast asleep there. In the house too, dead silence reigned."

"...all absorbing and invincible sleep,.."

"...everyone was lying stretched out side by side on the floor, on the benches, and in the passage. The children, left to their own devices, were crawling about and playing in the sand. The dogs, too, stole into their kennels, there being no one to bark at. One could walk through the house from one end to the other without meeting a soul; it would have been easy to steal everything and take it away in carts, if there were any thieves in those parts, for no one would have interfered with them. It was a sort of all-absorbing and invincible sleep, a true semblance of death. Everything was dead, except for the snoring that came in all sorts of tones and variations from every corner of the house."

"...everyone had his own fixed purpose in life!"

"..he looked at his surroundings, tasted the ephemeral good things of life, and calmed down, gazing dreamily at the evening sun going down slowly and quietly in the fiery conflagration of the sunset; at last he decided that his life had not turned out to be so simple and uncomplicated, but had been created and meant to be so in order to show that the ideally reposeful aspect of human existence was possible. It fell to the lot of other people, he reflected, to express its troubled aspects and set in motion the creative and destructive forces: everyone had his own fixed purpose in life! Such was the philosophy that the Plato of Oblomovka had worked out and that lulled him to sleep amidst the stern demands of duty and the problems of human existence! He was not born and educated to be a gladiator for the arena, but a peaceful spectator of the battle; his timid and indolent spirit could not have endured either the anxieties of happiness or the blows inflicted by life—therefore he merely gave expression to one particular aspect of it, and it was no use being sorry or trying to change it or to get more out of it."

"...felt at peace with himself only in his forgotten corner of the world"

"He looked upon his present way of life as a continuation of the same Oblomov-like-existence, except that he lived in a different place, and the times, too, were to a certain extent different. Here, too, as at Oblomovka, he managed to strike a good bargain with life, having obtained from it a guarantee of undisturbed peace. He triumphed inwardly at having escaped its annoying and agonizing demands and storms, which break from that part of the horizon where the lightnings of great joys flash and the sudden thunderclaps of great sorrows resound; where false hopes and magnificent phantoms of happiness are at play; where a man's own thought gnaws at his vitals and finally consumes him and passions kills; where man is engaged in a never-ceasing battle and leaves the battlefield shattered but still insatiate and discontented. Not having experienced the joys obtained by struggle, he mentally renounced them, and felt at peace with himself only in his forgotten corner of the world, where there is no struggle, no movement, and no life"

....he had always at his side an obedient and ready listener...."

"Oblomov put up with Alexeyev's visits......If he wanted to live in his own way.....lie without uttering a word, doze or pace the room—Alexeyev did not seem to be there at all; he too, was silent, dozing or pretending to read a book, or looking lazily at the pictures and knick-knack, yawning till tears came into his eyes. He could go on like that for three days on end. If,......Oblomov tired of being by himself and felt the need for expressing his thoughts, for talking, reading, arguing, showing emotion—he had always at his side an obedient and ready listener who shared with equal willingness his silence, his conversation, his excitement, and his trend of thoughts, whatever it might be."

✑

"Malinovka Heights"

Boris Pavlovich Raisky: a man at a turning point in life, looking back at his youth and feeling unsatisfied in his middle age. As a youth, he dreamed of distant lands which he never manages to visit in adulthood. He's unable to finish anything he's started and he's endlessly bored with almost everything. After his university studies and a short stint in the army and the civil service Raisky enjoys the life of an artist, frequenting St Petersburg's elegant circles, dabbing at his paintings, a little music, womanizing, and entertaining thoughts of writing a novel. But for a man like him, who has achieved nothing so far and by his own admission is "not born to work", the bustle of the capital proves too much, so he decides to visit his country estate of Malinovka. There he hopes to rediscover the joys of a simpler and more authentic life. But when he becomes emotionally involved with his beautiful cousin Vera and meets the dangerous freethinker Mark Volokhov, this results in a chain of events that lead to disappointment, confrontation and, ultimately, tragedy. The book explores themes of our dependence upon one another and the ways in which that dependence can consume us.

Passages from "Malinovka Heights"

"...the expression in his eyes would change from one moment to another ."

"At first glance, he appeared younger than his years. His broad white brow gleamed with a youthful freshness, and the expression in his eyes would change from one moment to another. At one moment they would be alive with thought, feeling and high spirits, and the very next moment would turn sombre and meditative, and then a moment later simply youthful, almost juvenile. At times, they would convey a mature, weary, abstracted impression typical of someone of his host's age. At the corners of his eyes there were even early traces of three crow's feet, ineradicable signs of age and experience. His straight black hair covered the back of his head and his ears, and a few silver strands flecked his temples. His cheeks as well as his brow still preserved the sheen of youth, especially around the eyes and mouth, but yellowish smudges could be discerned on his temples and chin.

Although it was not hard to detect from his features that he was at that time in life when youth had given up the struggle to fend off maturity, a time when a man has entered that second stage of life where every one of his experiences, feelings and ailments has left its mark one him. It was his mouth alone that had retained, in the barely perceptible movements of his delicate lips and his smile, a youthful, fresh and at times almost childlike expression ."

"...instinct was far more powerful than experience."

"..precocious sensitivity was not necessarily the fruit of experience. The ability to predict and anticipate the turns which life will take in the future is a quality of intuitive and observant people in general, but of women in particular, even without the experience to which instinct, a quality possessed by sensitive nature, serves as a precursor.

It prepares them for actual experience by means of clues of various kinds, which go undetected by simpler minds, but are apparent to open and sharper eyes, which in the time it takes for a single flash of lightning to break through the clouds, are capable of taking in the whole area it has illuminated and consigning it to their memory.

And it was eyes such as these that Vera possessed. All she had to do is to take one look at a crowd, in church, in the street, and was immediately able to pick out one given person, just as with a single glance at the Volga, she could take in a ship in one spot, a small boat in another, horses grazing on the island, the men towing a barge, a seagull, and smoke rising from a chimney in a distant village. And her mind was just as keen and sharp a her eyes and missed nothing…..Vera didn't know everything about the interplay of hearts and their struggles, but nevertheless it was apparent that she understood that therein lies a source of joy and sorrow, and that the mind, self-esteem, pride, embarrassment, are all swirling around in that whirlpool, and trouble the human being. In her, instinct was far more powerful than experience."

"Passion is unending intoxication,.."

"Passion is unending intoxication, without the undignified consequences of drunkenness," he went on. "There are always flowers underfoot. Before you stands an idol to which you want to pray, for which you would give your life. Stones may be weighing down your head, but in the throes of passion, you feel that you are being pelted by roses, you will take the grinding of teeth for music, the blows struck by a cherished hand will feel gentler than a mother's caress. Worries, life's troubles, all vanish—your life becomes one endless triumph, nothing but happiness looks upon you like this (he moved closer to her) and takes you by the hand (he took her hand) and your whole being thrills to the touch of fire and strength ."

"… she represses a smile, as if it were a sin."

"Tell me Granny, what is this Vera?"……. "You can see for yourself, what else can I tell you? She is what you see."…….. You see, her mind and her will are off limits. And if her grandmother were to dare ask her anything it would be 'No', 'it's nothing', 'I don't know','I've no idea'. "She was born into my hands, and she has spent her whole life with me, but I never know what's on her mind, or her likes and dislikes. Even if she's ill, you have no way of knowing; she never complains or ask for medicine —if anything, she's become even more taciturn. It's not that she's lazy, but she doesn't do anything; no sewing, no embroidery, doesn't even like music, and never goes to call on people—well, that's the kind of person she was born! I've never known her to laugh whole-heartedly, or to likely burst into tears. And even when she is amused, she represses a smile, as if it were a sin. And when there's something wrong, or she's upset, she immediately lock herself in her ivory tower to nurse her sorrow, and savour her joy. So there you are!"

"unbearable flashes of lightning and peals of thunder.."

"There was another flash of lightning and a long peal of thunder…..The rain was coming down in buckets; flashes of lightning followed one another in swift succession. Dusk and the thunder clouds plunged everything into darkness.

Raisky began to think better of his artistic impulse to go out and watch the storm because his umbrella had been soaked through by the downpour, and was letting in the rain which drenched his face and his clothing, and his feet were clogged with the soggy clay.....

Every minute he had to stop and wait for the next bolt of lightning before he could see enough to advance a few paces. He knew that somewhere at the bottom of the hill there was a pavilion from the time when the bushes and the trees had still formed part of the garden.

...recently, when he had been making his way to the river bank, he had happened to see it in the grove, but now he didn't know how to find it in order to take shelter, and from there perhaps to watch the storm.

The prospect of finding his way back through the bushes which grew close together and climbing up through the tussocks and holes in the ground was just too forbidding, and he decided to drag himself a further few hundred yards to the level terrain of the hillside and climb over the wattle fence, and ....follow the road to the village.

His boots were soaked through, and he could barely lift his feet out of the mud and tramp through the burdock and nettles,.....now he was not entirely indifferent to the unbearable flashes of lightning and peals of thunder overhead."

"what simplicity.....there is in his look and his manner."

"Ivan Ivanovich Tushin was youthful-looking. He was tall, broad-shouldered, well-built, and thirty-eight with thick, dark hair, strong features and big grey eyes, unpretentious and unassuming, even a little shy looking, and with a bushy dark beard. His hands were big and sunburned, but in proportion to his height, and with broad nails. He was dressed in a grey overcoat and a waistcoat buttoned to the neck surmounted by the turn-down collar of his shirt of home-spun cloth which fell over his tie. His gloves were of white suede and he was carrying a long riding crop with a silver handle.

A fine, strapping, youthful looking man; but what simplicity—to say the least —there is in his look and his manner."

"He listened with love in his heart...."

"....his heart skipped a beat at the mere prospect of passion and lurched at the thought of the delirious sensations that the future might hold for him. He listened with love in his heart at the rumbling of the distant thunder. He imagined the delight with which passion would break loose in him, how a raging fire would burn away the stagnation of his life, and a refreshing rain would irrigate the dried-up field and wash away the accumulated baggage of his past life."

☙

"The Same Old Story"

The story is set in the middle of the 19th century in the provincial estate of 20-year-old Alexander Aduev, a spoiled only son being fussed over by his silly, widowed mother as he prepares to leave for St Petersburg. Alexander doesn't exactly know what he's going to do in St Petersburg, other than, live the kind of life that involves writing poetry and becoming famous. Alexander has been spoiled all his life. His mother and servants have always attended to his every need. His mother and his first love, Sophia, have always praised his writing.

When he moves to St. Petersburg, however, Alexander suddenly learns that life is a lot more difficult. Alexander learns to leave some of his high expectations behinds and to realize that he doesn't have the talent to become an instant literary phenomenon or the patience to earn acclaim the hard way. However, he does discover that love, happiness, and emotion can make life worth living.

Passages from The "Same Old Story"

"It would even have been better for her to have loved him a little less,.."

"…that his mother, for all her loving care, was unable to provide him a proper perspective on life, and had failed to prepare him for the battles in store for him as they are for everyone. But for this she would have needed certain skills, sharper wits and a wealth of experience not limited by her narrow rural horizons. It would even have been better for her to have loved him a little less, not to have spent every minute of the day thinking about him, not to have spared him every possible trouble and unpleasantness, not to have done his weeping and suffering for him even in his childhood so as to give him a chance of developing a feeling for the prospect of adversity, and a chance to learn to muster his own resources and consider what lay ahead—in a word to realize that he was a man."

"Up in the dome, jackdaws cawed and sparrows chirped,.."

"A fresh breeze blew in through the iron grating into the window, lifting the cloth on the altar and rustling the grey hairs on the priest, turning the page of a book here and there and snuffing out a candle. The footsteps of the priest and the sexton rang out on the stone floor of the empty church. The sound of their voices echoed cheerlessly among the columns.

Up in the dome, jackdaws cawed and sparrows chirped, flying back and forth from one window to another, the flapping of their wings and the tolling of the bells sometimes drowning out the service…"

"his eyes would not let you see through them into his soul."

"He was not old, but was known rather as "a man in his prime"—somewhere between thirty-five and forty. As a matter of fact, he preferred to keep his age to himself, not as a matter of petty pride, but rather on account of a kind of careful calculation, as if he were bent on insuring his life on more advantageous terms. However, there was no suggestion that behind his reticence about his age there lurked some vanity, and that this reticence would somehow succeed in impressing the fair sex.

He was a tall, well-proportioned man with pronounced features set in a lusterless dark face. He moved with an even, graceful carriage, and his manner was reserved, but pleasant —the type who has usually described as a bel homme. His face conveyed the same element of reserve, of a kind of self-possession, and his eyes would not let you see through them into his soul."

"..as long as every joy, every happiness is granted you…"

"You're still young, how can you be expected to be as churchgoing as oldsters like us? I expect your duties will prevent you, and you'll stay up late in the company of your society friends, and get up late the next morning. God will be understanding because of your youth. But don't worry, you have a mother. She won't sleep late. As long as a drop of blood remains in my veins, my eyes can still shed tears, and

God tolerates my sins, if I don't have the strength to walk, I'll drag myself on my knees to the church door; I'll pray for your health, for your honours, promotions and decorations, and for every blessing that heaven and earth can bestow upon you. Surely Our Merciful Father will not reject the prayers of a poor old woman? I want nothing for myself. Let everything be taken from me, my health, my life, strike me blind, just as long as every joy, every happiness is granted you…"

"He dreamt of a tremendous passion which knew no obstacles"

"Nature, his mother's tender loving care, his nanny's veneration, and that of all the household servants, his soft bed, the delicious treats, the purring of Vaska—all those pleasures which are so highly valued in later years, he was happy to trade in for the unknown, an unknown fraught with a seductive and mysterious delight. Even Sofia's love, first love, tender and roseate was not enough to hold him back. What was that kind of love to him? He dreamt of a tremendous passion which knew no obstacles and crowned glorious exploits . The love he had for Sofia was a small thing compared with the great love yet to come. He dreamt also of the great services he would render his country. He had studied diligently and widely. His diploma stated that he was well versed in a dozen branches of knowledge, and half a dozen ancient and modern languages . But his greatest dream was that of becoming a famous writer. His friends were amazed by his poems. Before him there stretched any number of paths each more attractive than the last. He did not know in which direction to strike out. The only one he failed to see was the one straight ahead of him: if he had seen it, perhaps he might never have left."

"St. Petersburg resembled......those fairy-tale cities...."

"St. Petersburg was having one of its rare hot days. The sun brought the fields to life, but was having a deadening effect on the streets, heating the granite with its rays, bouncing off the stone and scorching passers-by. People were moving slowly with their heads down, and the dogs' tongues were hanging out. St. Petersburg resembled one of those fairy-tale cities where everything had suddenly been turned to stone with a wave of the wizard's wand. The carriages rumbled over the cobbles. Blinds were lowered over the windows like eyes which had been closed. The wooden-block paving gleamed like parquet floors and the heat underfoot burned the feet of pedestrians. The city was lifeless and sleepy."

CHAPTER TWO

Fyodor Mikhailovich Dostoyevsky (1821-81)

* *Novels deal with moral and philosophical questions: freedom of choice, Socialism, happiness, atheisms, good and evil.*
* *An addicted gambler who, after leaving Russia to avoid his creditors, lost all his money and wife's jewelry at a German casino.*
* *Writings emphasized the spiritual transformation of the individual.*
* *Published articles in a monthly journal that contained anti-Semantic views.*
* *Displayed a lifelong obsession with patricide.*
* *Arrested, prosecuted, and sentenced to death for reading a letter at a gathering of utopian socialists. Death sentence was commuted to four years of hard labor in Siberia.*
* *Asserted that the essence of life cannot be found by the reliance on intellect alone.*

"The Landlady"

Ordynov is a young man who has only learned of the world through books and academia and is completely naïve when it comes to people and very basic aspects of everyday life.

While wandering around St. Petersburg he becomes obsessed with a young woman in a church and follows her and the old man with her home. Since he is looking for new lodgings the young man is determined to get a room in the same house in which they lived. He eventually becomes their lodger and then is entangled in the strange circumstances surrounding the young woman and the old man. Katerina, the young woman might be mad or might be bewitched. The old man might be Katerina's husband, a mystic, a brigand, father, or a cousin who has taken her in. The story is a tale of love, murder, and sorcery full of twists and turns.

Passages from "The Landlady"

"..his eyes glittered with a hectic, inflamed light, haughty and staring."

"He raised his eyes, and was seized by an indescribable curiosity at the sight of these two strangers. They were an old man and a young woman. The old man was tall, still erect and vigorous, but emaciated and deathly pale. At first sight one might have taken him for a merchant visiting from some place far away. He wore a long, black fur caftan, which was evidently his Sunday best, and it was unfastened . Underneath the caftan another long-skirted Russian garment was visible, buttoned tightly all the way down. His bare necks carefully tied with a bright red kerchief; he was holding a fur hat. His long, straggling beard, which was half grey, reached down to his chest, and from under lowering beetle brows his eyes glittered with a hectic, inflamed light, haughty and staring."

"...that heart was ready at last either to break or find an outlet,.."

"Whether this extreme sensitivity to impressions, this defenselessness and vulnerability had been nurtured by solitude; whether such impetuosity of heart had been prepared in the agonizing, airless and claustrophobic silence of long, sleepless nights, amidst the unconscious yearnings and impatient convulsions of the spirit, until that heart was ready at last either to break or find an outlet, and simply had no alternative but to pour itself out——as when on a sweltering, sultry day the sky suddenly turns black and a thunderstorm pours rain and fire on to the parched earth, hanging raindrops on the emerald boughs like pearls, trampling the grass and the fields, and beating down to the earth the tender chalices of the flowers, so that afterwards everything can revive once more in the sun's first rays, surging and rising towards it and majestically wafting to the sky its sweet, luxurious incense, rejoicing and exulting in its new lease of life…"

"…he was poor, and rented rooms were expensive."

"His landlady, the very poor, elderly widow of a government clerk, from whom he rented lodgings, had been compelled by unforeseen circumstances to move out of St. Petersburg and go and live with relatives somewhere in the wilds—and this she had done without waiting for the first of the month, when his rent was due.

And he spent the remaining days in his accustomed refuge, the young man had surveyed it with regret, feeling a sense of vexation at having to abandon it; he was poor, and rented rooms were expensive. The day after his landlady's departure, he had taken his cap and set off wandering through the lanes of St. Petersburg, studying all the advertisements that were fixed to the gates of the houses, and selected the darkest, most crowded and most *solidly built* tenements, where there was the greatest likelihood of finding a corner in this room of some poor lodgers."

"..his mother leaned over him,....
kissing him and lulling.."

"….there would seem to begin for him once again the soft, tranquil years of his early childhood with their luminous joy, their inextinguishable happiness, their first sweet wonder at life, their hosts of radiant spirits which flew out from every flower he plucked, which played with him on the succulent green meadow in front of the little house surrounded with acacia, which smiled to him from the crystal waters of the vast lake by which he sat for hours on end, listening to wave lapping upon wave, and which rustled about him with their wings, lovingly strewing his little cradle-cot with bright, rainbow-coloured dreams, as his mother leaned over him, making the sign of the cross over him, kissing him and lulling him to sleep with a quiet lullaby in the long, peaceful nights. But then, suddenly, a being had started to appear which had disturbed him with an unchildlike horror, and had infused his life with the first, slow poison of bitterness and tears,.."

"…he surveyed the faces of the passers-by
with a thoughtful gaze,.."

"….he read the scene that brightly unfolded before him as if it were a book, between the lines. Everything had an effect on him; he did not miss a single impression and he surveyed the faces of the passers-by with a thoughtful gaze, studied the physiognomy of everyone around him, and listened with affection to the talk of the ordinary people as though in everything he were finding the verification of the conclusions he had reached in the silence of his solitary nights. Often some trivial detail would strike him, giving rise to an idea, and for the first time he started to feel annoyed for having buried himself alive in his cell in the way he had done. Here everything moved faster; his pulse was firm and quick, his intelligence, which had been stifled by solitude, and was sharpened and ennobled only by intense, exalted activity, now functioned swiftly, calmly and boldly. What was more, he had conceived an unconscious desire somehow to squeeze himself into this life which was alien to him and whose existence he had until this moment only known or, rather, sensed with the instinct of an artist."

಄

"White Nights"

This is the story of an innocent young man and the love he feels for a woman he meets on the streets of St. Petersburg. The young man suffers from loneliness. In the last two weeks of every June, St. Petersburg experiences one of its most celebrated natural phenomena - the White Nights, a time of near-midnight sun. While wandering the longly streets of Moscow during one of these White Nights, the solitary young man encounters a crying young woman. This encounter sparks an intense four nights in which they reveal themselves to each other in dramatic monologues. He gets to know and falls in love with the young woman, but the love remains unreturned, as the woman is finally united with her one true love.

Passages from "White Nights"

"May your sky be always clear"

"But that I should feel any resentment against you, Nastenka! That I should cast a dark shadow over your bright, serene happiness! That I should chill and darken your heart with bitter reproaches, wound it with secret remorse, cause it to beat anxiously at the moment of bliss! That I should crush a single one of those delicate blooms which you will wear in your dark hair when you walk up the aisle to the altar with him! Oh no—never, never! May your sky be always clear, may your dear smile be always bright and happy, and may you be for ever [sic] blessed for that moment of bliss and happiness which you gave to another lonely and grateful heart! Good Lord, only a moment of bliss! Isn't such a moment sufficient for the whole of a man's life?"

"..those sad and wistful eyes blaze forth with such a fire?"

"There is something indescribably moving in the way nature in Petersburg, suddenly with the coming of spring, reveals herself in all her might and glory, in all the splendour with which heaven has endowed her, in the way she blossoms out, dresses up, decks herself out with flowers…She reminds me somehow rather forcibly of that girl, ailing and faded, upon whom you sometimes look with pity or with a certain compassionate affection, or whom you simply do not notice at all, but who in the twinkling of an eye and only for one fleeting moment becomes by some magic freak of chance indescribably fair and beautiful; and stunned and fascinated, you ask yourself what power it was that made those sad and wistful eyes blaze forth with such a fire?"

"…the beauty, so momentarily evoked,….faded so quickly…"

"..the brief moment passes, and tomorrow perhaps you will again encounter the same wistful and forlorn gaze, the same wan face, the same resignation and diffidence in her movements, and, yes, even remorse, even traces of some benumbing vexation and despondency for that brief outburst of passion. And you feel sorry that the beauty, so momentarily evoked, should have faded so quickly and so irrevocably, that she should have burst upon your sight so deceptively and to so little purpose—that she should not have given you time even to fall in love with her..."

"...it is...her duty as a woman not to reject.....an unhappy man like me,..."

"I longed to talk to a society lady in the street, I mean, talk to her when she was alone, and without any formality. Very humbly, of course, very respectfully, very passionately. Tell her how horribly depressed I am by my lonely life; ask her not to send me away; explain to her that I have no other way of knowing what a woman is like; suggest to her that it is really her duty as a woman not to reject the humble entreaty of an unhappy man like me, finally, explain to her that all I want of her is that she should say a few friendly words to me, say them with sympathy and understanding,...."

".. she comforted and soothed my heart!."

"But how beautiful people are when they are gay and happy! How brimful of love their hearts are! It is as though they wanted to pour their hearts into the heart of another human being, as though they wanted the whole world to be gay and laugh with them. And how infectious that gaiety is! There was so much joy in her words yesterday, so much goodness in her heart towards me. How sweet she was to me, how hard she tried to be nice to me, how she comforted and soothed my heart! Oh, how sweet a woman can be to you when she is happy! And I? Why, I was completely taken in. I thought she—-"

"Notes From The Underground"

The unnamed narrator, a retired civil servant living in St. Petersburg, is a former official who has defiantly withdrawn into an underground existence. Describing himself as a sick, spiteful, and unattractive man, his thoughts and moods veer unpredictably as he reflects on the folly of idealism and the reality of human squalor and degradation. In full retreat from society, he scrawls a passionate, obsessive, self-contradictory narrative that serves as a devastating attack on social utopianism and an assertion of man's essentially irrational nature.

Passages from "Notes From The Underground"

"... no man ever knowingly acts against his own interests..."

"Oh tell me who was it first said, who was it first proclaimed that the only reason man behaves dishonourably is because he does not know his own interests, and that if he were enlightened, if his eyes were opened to his real normal interests, he would at once cease behaving dishonourably and would at once become good and honourable because, being enlightened and knowing what is good for him, he would see that his advantage lay in doing good, and of course it is well known that no man ever knowingly acts against his own interests and therefore he would, as it were, willy-nilly start doing good."

"Love is a mystery that God alone only comprehends…"

"….no one ought to know what passes between man and wife, if they love one another. And however much they quarrel, they ought not to call in their own mother to adjudicate between them, and to tell tales of one another. They are their own judges. Love is a mystery that God alone only comprehends and should be hidden from all eyes whatever happens. If that is done, it is more holy, and better. They are more likely to respect one another, and a lot depends on their respect for one another. And if once there has been love, if at first they married for love, there is no reason why their love should pass away."

"The street-lamps twinkled desolately and uselessly…"

"A moment later I began to dress madly, putting on hurriedly whatever clothes I could lay my hands on, and rushed headlong after her. She had hardly had time to walk more than a hundred yards when I ran out into the street.

The street was quiet and deserted. It was snowing heavily, the snowflakes falling almost perpendicularly and piling up in deep drifts on the pavement and on the empty road. There was not a soul to be seen, not a sound to be heard. The street-lamps twinkled desolately and uselessly, I ran about a hundred yards to the cross-roads and stopped.

Where had she gone? And why was I running after her?"

"…. if you're so utterly without shame!"

"I stood there utterly humiliated. The whole party left the room noisily. Trudolyubov began singing some stupid song. Simonov stayed behind for a second to tip the waiters. I suddenly went up to him. "Simonov," I said firmly and desperately, "let me have six roubles!"

He gazed at me in utter amazement, with a sort of stupefied look in his eyes. He, too, was drunk. "But you're not coming there with us, are you?" "Yes, I am!" "I haven't any money!" He snapped out with a contemptuous grin, and left the room. I caught him by the overcoat. It was a nightmare. "Simonov, I saw you had money. Why do you refuse me? Am I a scoundrel? Be careful how you refuse me: if you knew, if you knew why I'm asking! Everything depends on it, my whole future, all my plans!…."

Simonov took out the money and almost flung it at me. "Take it if you're so utterly without shame!" he said, pitilessly, and rushed away to overtake them."

"… street-lamps flickered….in the snowy haze"

"The wet snow was falling in large flakes. I unbuttoned my overcoat —I didn't mind the snow. I forgot everything, for I had finally made up my mind to slap Zverkov in the face, and I couldn't help feeling with horror that now it was going to happen for certain and that nothing in the world could stop it. Solitary street-lamps flickered gloomily in the snowy haze like torches at a funeral. The snow was drifting under my overcoat, under my coat, and under my collar where it melted. I did not button myself up: all was lost, anyway!"

∽

"The Brothers Karamazov"

Set in 19th-century Russia, *T*he Brothers Karamazov takes place in the era of the 1860s, shortly after the emancipation of the serfs in 1861 and the judicial reforms of 1864. The setting is an obscure country town somewhere in Russia. This philosophical novel explores the interrelation between God, free will, and ethics through the lives of four half-brothers

The titular brothers Karamazov are Dmitri, Ivan, Alyosha, and Smerdyakov, who are the sons of the town reprobate. The novel follows the circumstances leading up to the murder of the brothers' father Fyodor, and the subsequent arrest of one of them for the crime. As the narrative follows an investigation of the father's murder, each brother presents a different inflection of humanity—from passionate spiritualism to unyielding skepticism.

Passages from The Brothers Karamazov

"… it was already deep twilight, but the rooms had not yet been lit."

"When Rakitin and Alyosha went in to see her it was already deep twilight, but the rooms had not yet been lit. Grushenka herself lay in her sitting-room on her large, ungainly sofa with its back of red mahogany, hard and upholstered in leather that had long since worn away and gathered holes. Under her head she had the two white down pillows from her bed. She was dressed up, as though she were expecting someone, in a black silk dress and a thin lace *naolka,* which thoroughly suited her; over her shoulders was thrown a lace scarf that was pinned in place with a massive gold brooch. She was indeed waiting for someone, lay almost in anguish and impatience, her face slightly pale, with hot lips and eyes, as she tapped the tip of her right foot impatiently against the sofa's arm."

"...Let us drink to life, friend brother!"

"I love life, I have loved life too much, so much that it's positively loathsome. Enough! To life, my dear fellow, to life let us drink, to life do I propose a toast! Why am I so pleased with myself? I am base, but am pleased with myself. And yet, I'm tormented by the fact that I am base, but pleased with myself. I bless creation, am this moment ready to bless God and his creation, but... I must exterminate a certain stinking insect, so that it does not go creeping about, does not spoil life for others... Let us drink to life, friend brother! What can be more dear than life? Nothing, nothing! To life and to a certain empress of empresses! "

"... his face, ...produced a painful impression:"

"Ivan Fyodorovich made his approach with a slowness that was somehow astonishing, without looking at anyone and even with his head lowered, as though he were frowningly reflecting on something. His dress was immaculate, but his face, on me at any rate, produced a painful impression: there was in it something that was almost touched with earth, something that resembled the face of one who is dying. His eyes were dull; he raised them and slowly surveyed the chamber with them."

"... imparted to his entire countenance a .....malign and irritable aspect."

"The old man sat alone at the table, in slippers and an old topcoat, looking over some sort of accounts, for the sake of diversion, though without great attentiveness. He was completely alone in the whole house........But it was not the accounts that were on his mind. Though he had risen early that morning and had endeavoured to maintain his spirits, he none the less had a tired and enfeebled look. His brow, on which overnight enormous purple bruises had spread, was swathed in a red handkerchief. His nose had also swollen powerfully overnight, and on it there had also formed a number of blotchy bruises which, though inconsiderable, somehow nevertheless decidedly imparted to his entire countenance a particularly malign and irritable aspect. The old man knew this and…. gave…an unfriendly glare."

"…..'smite each and every heart with unknown power'"

"Everything grew quiet as the first words of the celebrated orator rang out. The entire chamber glued its eyes upon him. He began exceedingly directly, in a simple and convinced manner, but without the slightest arrogance. There was not the slightest attempt at eloquence, at notes of pathos, at words that rang with emotion. This was a man who had begun to speak within an intimate circle of people who were sympathetic to him. His voice was magnificent, loud and likeable, (sic) and even in this voice alone one seemed to hear something sincere and open-hearted. All, however, came to grasp at once that orator could suddenly rise to genuine pathos— and 'smite each and every heart with unknown power'."

CHAPTER THREE

Ivan Turgenev (1818-83)

* *Master of storytelling, style, and language known for his detailed descriptions about everyday life in 19th century Russia.*
* *Held a nonjudgmental, but somewhat pessimistic view of the world.*
* *Served a one month detention and eighteen months of house arrest for expressing his views on reforming Russian society.*
* *Believed that Russia needed to Westernize.*
* *Expressed his admiration for nature through detailed descriptions of colors, sounds, and scents.*
* *In a letter to a friend he noted, "On certain days I feel crushed by this burden. It seems to me that I have no more marrow in my bones, and I carry on like an old post horse, worn out but courageous."*

"Sketches from a Hunter's Album"

Based on his own observations riding around his family's estate, Turgenev's stories explore the difficult lives of the peasants and the Russian system of serfdom. The album is filled with moving insights into the lives of peasants and landowners, doctors and bailiffs, neglected wives and bereft mothers - each providing a glimpse of love, tragedy, courage and loss. The stories describes scenes of naturalistic sketches and everyday lives of serfs, and fellow land owners, as well as the injustices and contradictions of the social system of serfdom.

Passages from "Sketches from a Hunter's Album"

"The pale-grey sky shone bright and cold.."

"A current of fresh air brushed my face. I opened my eyes to see that morning was beginning. As yet there was no sign of dawn's pinkness, but in the east it had begun to grow light. The surrounding scene became visible, if only dimly. The pale-grey sky shone bright and cold and tinged with blue; stars either winked their faint light or faded; the ground was damp and leaves were covered with the sweat of dew, here and there sounds of life, voices could be heard, and a faint, light wind of early morning began its wandering and fleet-footed journey across the earth. My body responded to it with a mild, joyful shivering."

"....suddenly he'd give a sign and sink into an armchair..."

"In people who are constantly and strongly preoccupied by one thought or by a single passion there is always some common feature noticeable, some common likeness in behaviour, no matter how different their qualities, their abilities, their position in society and their education. The longer I observed Radilov, the more it seemed to me that he belonged to such a category of person. He would talk about running his estate, about the harvest, about the haymaking, about the war, about the provincial gossip and forthcoming elections, he would talk quite freely, even with a sense of involvement, but suddenly he'd give a sign and sink into an armchair, dry- washing his face like a man worn out by hard work. It seemed his entire spirit, kindly and warm though it was, was penetrated, permeated through and through, by a singe feeling."

"Suddenly, behind us, there came a noise from the creek..."

"...even in the shade it was stifling. The heavy, heat-laden wind had literally fallen to nothing and one's burning face sought any kind of breeze, but there was no breeze at all. The sun literally beat down from a blue, darkened sky. Directly opposite us, on the other bank, a field of oats glowed yellow, with wormwood growing in it here and there, and yet not a single stalk so much as quivered. A little lower down a peasant's horse stood in the river up to its knees and lazily waved about its wet tail. Occasionally a large fish swam to the surface beneath an overhanging bush, emitted bubbles and then slowly sank to the bottom, leaving behind it a slight ripple. Grasshoppers sawed away in the sun-browned grass. Quail cried out as if despite themselves. Hawks floated smoothly above the fields and frequently stopped in one spot, rapidity beating their wings and fanning out their tails. We sat motionless, oppressed by the heat. Suddenly, behind us, there came a noise from the creek as someone descended towards the spring."

"....the air was full of suffocating dust."

"It was an intolerably hot July day when, slowly dragging one foot after another, I and my dog climbed up the hill beside the Kolotovka ravine in the direction of The Welcome tavern. The sun blazed in the sky, as if fit to explode; it steamed and baked everything remorselessly, and the air was full of suffocating dust. Glossy-feathered rooks and crows hung their beaks and gazed miserably at those who passed by, as if literally imploring their sympathy. Only the sparrows kept their spirits up and, spreading their feathers, chirruped away more fiercely than ever, squabbled round the fences, took off in flight from the dusty roadway and soared in grey clouds above the plantations of green hemp. I was tormented by thirst. There was no water to be got close by: in Kolotovka, as in so many other steppe villages, the peasants, for want of springs and wells, are accustomed to drink a kind of liquid mud from the ponds.....But who would call that beastly drink water?"

".... the air is impregnated with the flesh bitter-sweet fragrance..."

"And a summer morning in July! Has anyone save a hunter ever experienced the delight of wandering through bushes at dawn? Your feet leave green imprints in the grass that is heavy and white with dew. You push aside wet bushes—the warm scent accumulated in the night almost smothers you; the air is impregnated with the flesh bitter-sweet fragrance of wormwood, the honeyed scent of buckwheat and clover; far-off an oak forest rises like a wall, shining purple in the sunshine; the air is still fresh, but the coming heat can already be felt. Your head becomes slightly dizzy from such an excess of sweet scents. And there's no end to the bushes...Away in the distance ripening rye glows yellow and there are narrow strips of rust-red buckwheat. Then there's the sound of a cart;..."

⟡

"Home of the Gentry"

This is a story about the homecoming of a young member of the upper class, who, broken and disillusioned by a failed marriage, returns to his estate and finds love again - only to lose it. The sense of loss and of unfulfilled promise reflects the theme that humanity is not destined to experience happiness except as something ephemeral and inevitably doomed. The homecoming also represents a whole generation of young Russians who have fallen under the spell of European ideas that have uprooted them from Russia, but have proved ultimately superfluous. In tragic bewilderment, they attempt to find reconciliation with the land and culture of their birth.

Passages from "Home of the Gentry"

".... fresh, lush nakedness and wilderness of the steppe,..."

"Laying his head back on a cushion and folding his arms, Lavretsky gazed at the rows of fields which passed in a fan-wise movement, at the willows which slowly passed into and out of sight, at the stupid rooks and crows which looked out of the corners of their eyes in dull suspiciousness at the passing carriage, at the long boundaries between the fields overgrown with ragwort, wormwood and field rowans; he gazed... and this fresh, lush nakedness and wilderness of the steppe, this greenery, these long low hills, the ravines with their ground-hugging clumps of oak trees, the grey little villages, the flowing shapes of birches— the whole of this picture of Russia, which he had not seen for so long, evoked in him sweet and simultaneously anguished feelings and oppressed his heart with a kind of pleasant sadness. His thoughts took a slow wandering course; their outlines were as vague and troubled as the outlines of those high and also seemingly wandering clouds."

"... her bony hand ceaselessly emerging from her coat.."

"Worshippers arrived one by one, stopped, crossed themselves and bowed on all sides; their footsteps made a ringing sound in the emptiness and quiet, clearly echoing the vaulted roof. A decrepit old woman in a threadbare coat with a hood kneeled…and prayed diligently; her toothless, yellow, wrinkled face expressed intense exultation; her reddened eyes gazed immovably up at the icons on the iconostasis; her bony hand ceaselessly emerging from her coat and slowly and firmly made the sign of the cross in broad large gestures. A peasant with a thick beard and despondent face, disheveled and crumpled, entered the church, fell at once on both knees and instantly began hurriedly crossing himself, throwing back and shaking his head after each obeisance. Such bitter sorrow was written in his face and expressed in all his movements…"

"…now understood why life was worth living.."

"Late in the evening Lavretsky returned home and sat for a long while without undressing, his hand over his eyes, in an ecstasy of wonder. It seemed to him that he had only now understood why life was worth living; all his presuppositions and intentions, all that stuff and nonsense, vanished in a flash; his entire soul blended into one feeling, into one desire—a desire for happiness, for possession of love, a woman's sweet love."

"Traces of human life vanish very quickly:.."

"Having looked over the house, Lavretsky went into the garden and was satisfied by what he saw. It was entirely overgrown with thick weeds and burdock and gooseberry and raspberry bushes; but there was much shade and many old limes which were striking for their hugeness and the curious arrangements of their boughs, the result of having been planted too close together and —perhaps a hundred years ago—severely pruned back. The garden ended in a small bright pond with a fringe of tall reddish reeds. Traces of human life vanish very quickly: Glafira Petrovna's estate had not yet gone wild, but it seemed already to have sunk into that quiet repose, which possesses everything on earth wherever there is no restless human infection to affect it."

"The stars disappeared in a bright haze;.."

"The charm of the summer night possessed him; everything around him seemed so unexpectedly strange and at the same time so long and so sweetly familiar to him; near and far—and one could see a long way, although the eye could not distinguish much of what it saw—everything was at peace; this very peace was redolent of youth bursting with life. Lavretsky's horse stepped out, rocking him evenly from side to side; its large black shadow moved along beside it; there was something secretly pleasing in the tramp of its hooves, something joyous and wonderful in the ringing cries of the quail. The stars disappeared in a bright haze; the moon, not yet full, shone with a hard glow; its light flowed in a pale-blue stream across the sky and fell in patches of smoky gold on the light clouds which passed close to it; the freshness of the air brought a slight moisture to the eyes, gently caressed the limbs and flowed freely into the lungs."

∽

"Fathers and Sons"

Set against the backdrop of serfs' emancipation, new liberal ideas, and other changes in Russia's social and political climate, the fathers of two sons try to come to grips with their sons' newfound political and philosophical ideologies. For their part the sons struggle to reconcile the belief that morality, tradition, and authority have no purpose with their newfound emotion: love. The story involves or addresses the generation gap created as individual families and the whole of Russia accepts or rejects new ideas.

Passages from "Fathers and Sons"

"... a long village stretched out in two rows of houses..."

"The estate...stood on a bare sloping hill a short distance from a yellow stone church with a green roof, white pillars and a fresco painting over the main entrance depicting 'The Resurrection of Christ' in a so-called Italian manner. Particularly remarkable....was a swarthy warrior in a spiked helmet spreadeagled in the foreground. Behind the church a long village stretched out in two rows of houses with chimneys visible here and there among the straw roofs. The manor house was built in the same style as the church, a style known among us as belonging to the age of Alexander I. The house was also painted yellow and had a green roof, white pillars and a pediment bearing a coat of arms."

"... skylarks poured out their song in unending, resonant streams."

"....spring began to come into its own. Everything around glinted green and gold, everything softly and expansively waved and shone under the quiet breath of a warm breeze, everything —the trees, the bushes, the grass. Everywhere skylarks poured out their song in unending, resonant streams. Lapwings cried as they circled above the low-lying meadows or ran about silently among the tufts of grass. Rooks wandered about, darkening beautifully among the soft green of the low spring wheat and disappeared in the rye, which was already beginning to whiten, their heads showing here and there among its smoky waves."

"The entire outward appearance …..so elegant and well-bred,…"

"…at that moment there entered the drawing room a man of average height, dressed in a dark English suit, a fashionably low-hanging cravat and patent-leather shoes:…. To all appearances he was about forty-five. His short-cut grey hair shone with a dark brilliance like new silver. His face, looking peevish but devoid of wrinkles, was unusually regular and pure of line, as if literally carved by a delicate and fluent scalpel, and retained traces of remarkable beauty; particularly striking were the bright, dark, elongated eyes. The entire outward appearance …..so elegant and well-bred, preserved a youthfulness of figure and an upward striving, away from the earth, which tends for the greater part to vanish after one's twenties."

"… there arose in the midst of the fine spring day…"

"….all the peasants they came across were in ragged clothes and riding clapped-out nags. The roadside willows were like beggars in tatters with torn bark and broken branches. Emaciated, rough-coated, almost bare bones, cows hungrily munched at the grass in ditches. It was as if they'd only just that minute escaped from the clutches of some fearful, deadly claws—and, summoned into being by the miserable sight of these enfeebled cattle, there arose in the midst of the fine spring day the white spectre (sic) of endless, joyless winter with its blizzards, frosts and snows…."

"… while at night she would cry and pray and find no peace of mind anywhere…"

"…occasional appearances were made in St. Petersburg society by a lady who has not been forgotten to this day,….She had a well-educated and decent but rather silly husband, and no children. She would suddenly go abroad, suddenly return to Russia, and in general led a strange life. She was considered a feather-brained coquette, used to devote herself zestfully to all manner of pleasures, would dance herself off her feet and laugh and joke with young men whom she would receive before dinner in the half-light of her drawing-room, while at night she would cry and pray and find no peace of mind anywhere and frequently spend her time till morning wandering about her room sorrowfully wringing her hands or sitting, all pale and cold, over a psalter. Day would dawn and she would be transformed once again into a society lady and once more she would go out and laugh and chatter and literally hurl herself at whatever might afford her the slightest pleasure."

∽

"Virgin Soil"

The novel depicts a group of the young people in late nineteenth century Russia who reject the standard cultural mores of their time and join a movement of political activists. They reject their lives of affectation and luxury and 'go amongst the people', to live the lives of simple workers and peasants in order to sow the seeds of revolution in the virgin soil of the Russian peasantry.

Passages from "Virgin Soil"

".. from doors suddenly flung open came blasts of dirty heat,.."

"It was Saturday night: there were no passers-by in the streets, but the taverns were still crowded. Hoarse voices, drunken songs, the nasal whine of concertinas came from them in bursts; from doors suddenly flung open came blasts of dirty heat, the acrid smell of spirits, the red glow of night lights. In front of almost every tavern stood peasant carts, harnessed to shaggy, pot-bellied nags; with their tousled heads drooping submissively, they appeared to be sleeping. A ragged, unbelted peasant in a large winter cap, which hung like a sack over the back of his neck, would emerge from the tavern and, leaning with his chest against the shafts, remain motionless, feebly and fumblingly moving his hands; or a haggard factory worker, his cap askew, his nankeen shirt hanging loose, his feet bare—his boots having remained in the drinking establishment—would take a few hesitant steps, halt, scratch his back and, with a sudden groan, go back again."

"….but nowhere was there any sign of neatness, precision or even tidiness; on the contrary,.."

"The factory was evidently flourishing and working flat out; from all parts came the purposeful rumble and roar of ceaseless activity. Machines snorted and clanked, looms creaked, wheels hummed, belts slapped, barrows, barrels and loaded carts rolled along and disappeared. The sound of shouted orders, bells and whistles rang out. Workmen in belted shirts, their hair in bandanas, and working girls wearing print dresses, ran quickly by. Horses in harness moved off. A thousand-headed human force, stretched to the utmost, droned all around. Everything proceeded in orderly, rational fashion, at full throttle, but nowhere was there any sign of neatness, precision or even tidiness; on the contrary, everywhere one was struck by casualness, dirt and soot. Here a window pane smashed; there plaster was peeling, boards were loose, a door yawned wide open; in the middle of the main courtyard was a large black puddle with an iridescent sheen of decay; beyond it were heaps of discarded bricks; remnants of sacking, matting, wooden drawers and bits of rope lay strewn about; shaggy dogs with tight bellies wandered about, not even barking; in a corner, under a fence, sat a boy of about four, bespattered with soot, his belly distended and his hair dishevelled (sic). He sat and wept in despair, as if the whole world had abandoned him; next to him, smeared with the same soot, a pig, surrounded by a motley litter of piglets, was guzzling cabbage heads; ragged underwear fluttered on a taut line. A stifling stench everywhere! A Russian factory—unmistakably—not a German nor yet a French manufactory. "

"… he conversed in a strange language which purported to be French."

"He did not improve on his father's fortune, being, as the saying goes, a joueur, a Russian-style epicurean, with no business sense at all. He was a man of about forty, somewhat stout, ugly, pockmarked, with small porcine eyes; he spoke very rapidly, mangling his words in the process, waved his arms, criss-crossed his legs, giggled, in general giving the impression on being gormless, spoilt and extremely vain. He considered himself an educated man, dressed German-style and lived in a slovenly but expansive fashion, had rich acquaintances, with whom he conversed in a strange language which purported to be French."

"… to left and right everything was being masked.."

"Low clouds covered the sky and, although it was not totally dark and the flattened ruts on the road could be seen ahead, glinting palely, to left and right everything was being masked and the outlines of separate objects merged into large, indistinct patches. It was a dim, treacherous night; the wind came in intermittent damp squalls, bringing with it the smell of both rain and fields of corn. When, after passing an oak sapling which served as a landmark, they had to turn on to a byway, things grew even more difficult; at times the narrow track disappeared completely: The coachman proceeded more slowly."

"…everything was moving, everything was fluttering."

"It was typical June weather, although fresh: high clouds moving skittishly over a blue sky, a strong, steady wind, a road, its dust laid by the previous day's rain, willows rustling, glinting, rippling—everything was moving, everything was fluttering. The weak whistling call of quails was heard coming from distant hills, across green ravines, as if it had wings on which it was flying; rooks looked glossy in the sunshine; something moved like black fleas along the level line of the bare horizon—it was peasants ploughing their fallow land for a second time."

CHAPTER FOUR

Mikhail Lermontov (1814-1841)

* An avid admirer of Pushkin who described him (Lermontov) as, "..a very great talent."
* Expressed concern about "Being able to be creative and being able to be creative constantly ."
* Arrested and reassigned to a military regiment in the Caucasus for criticizing the monarchy.
* Writing style is misty, mysterious, sparkling, fresh and reflect the influence of the German Classical tradition on Russia.
* Wrote with the aim of transforming the way Russians saw themselves .

"A Hero of Our Time"

The story is set in the Russian Caucasus Mountains during the 1830s. Grigory Pechorin, the anti-hero, is a bored, self-centered, and cynical young army officer who, with impunity, toys with the love of women and the goodwill of men. He impulsively undertakes dangerous adventures, risks his life, and destroys women who care for him. Although he is capable of feeling deeply, Pechorin prefers to wasted his gifts, display cynicism, and fulfill his desire for any kind of action-good or ill-that will stave off boredom

Passages from "A Hero of Our Time"

"The air was vibrant with electricity."

"I got up late today, and when I got to the well, there was no one there. It was getting hot. Small fluffy white clouds were racing in from the snowy mountains, giving promise of a storm. The summit of Mashuk smoked like an extinguished torch, and wisps of grey cloud coiled and slid round it like snakes, as though entangled and held back by the thorny scrub. The air was vibrant with electricity."

"Why was she here? And was it her?"

"I went into the vine walk that leads to the grotto. I felt sad, thinking of the young woman with the mole on her cheek that Werner had told me about. Why was she here? And was it her? And why did I think it was her? Why was I even sure of it? There are plenty of women with moles on their cheeks. It was with these thoughts going through my mind that I came to the grotto. A woman was sitting on a stone seat in the cool shade of its vault. She wore a straw hat and was wrapped in a black shawl. Her head was sunk on her breast, her face hidden by her hat. Not wishing to disturb her meditation, I was about to turn back, when she glanced up at me"

".. my coolness and self-control vanished,.."

"I was left alone in the steppe, my last hope gone. I tried walking, but my legs gave way beneath me. Worn out by the excitements of the day and my sleepless night, I fell down on the wet grass and wept like a child. I lay there a long time, weeping bitterly, not attempting to hold back the tears and sobs. I thought my chest would burst. All my coolness and self-control vanished, my heart wilted, reason deserted me.

Anyone seeing me at that moment would have turned away in contempt."

"… dark and radiant images traced by my restless, eager fancy."

"Many similar thoughts ran through my mind, but I didn't dwell on them, for I'm not given to brooding on abstract ideas. It gets you nowhere. As a boy I was a dreamer and dwelt with loving care on the dark and radiant images traced by my restless, eager fancy. And what did it bring me? Weariness, as though I'd spent a night wrestling a phantom, and a vague, regretful memory. In this fruitless struggle I wasted all the ardour (sic) and drive that are needed in real life, and when I came to life itself, I had been through everything mentally before and found it boring and disgusting, like reading a poor pastiche of a long familiar book."

"… men who imagined the stars took part in men's petty squabbles.."

"I walked home through the empty back streets of the village. A full red moon was just showing over the broken line of buildings, like the glare of a fire. Stars shone calmly in the deep blue sky, and I was amused to think that there, were once wise men who imagined the stars took part in men's petty squabbles over a patch of land or somebody's 'rights'. While in fact these lamps, which they supposed had been lit for the sole purpose of shining on their battles and triumphs, still burn on as bright as ever, while they, with all their passions and hopes, have long since vanished, like a fire lit by some carefree traveller(sic) at the edge of a forest. Yet what strength they derived from this certainty that the heavens with all their countless hosts looked down on them in silent, but never-failing sympathy."

⚬〰⚬

Stanzas from Various Poems

Lermontov was by nature a rather secretive person. He did not know how to maintain a secular conversation at the proper level and reward women with flattering compliments. When etiquette demanded, he became sharp and mocking which resulted in his acquiring the reputation as an ill-mannered rude person who despises etiquette. Consequently, he expressed his thoughts, feelings, and observations in a wide collection of poems.

"Farewell"

Farewell! Nevermore shall we meet, we shall never touch hands—so farewell! Your heart is now free, but in none will it ever be happy to dwell.

One moment together we came: time eternal is nothing to this! All senses we suddenly drained, burned all in the flame of one kiss. Farewell! And be wise, do not grieve: our love was short for regret, and hard as we found it to part harder still would it be if we met.

"My Native Land"

If I do love my land, strangely I love it: 'tis something reason cannot cure. Glories of war I do not covet, but neither peace proud and secure, nor the mysterious past and dim romances can spur my soul to pleasant fancies.

And still I love thee—why I hardly know: I love thy fields

so coldly meditative, native dark swaying woods and native rivers that sea-like foam and flow.

In a clattering cart I love to travel on country roads: watching the rising star, yearning for sheltered sleep, my eyes unravel the trembling lights of sad hamlets afar….

"All Alone I Walk Upon the Roadway" (three stanzas)

All alone I walk upon the roadway, Mistborne whitened glimmers in my view, Night is still, to God the desert listens, And the stars are talking in the blue.

All the heavens breathe in solemn wonder, All the earth is lost in dark blue light. Do I wait for something in the darkness? Do I mourn for some forlorn delight?

Nay, I wait for nothing in the darkness, And I mourn for nothing in the past. All I ask is freedom and oblivion, All I seek is but to sleep at last……

"On the Death of Pushkin" (one stanza)

He fell, a slave of tinsel-honour, A sacrifice of slander's lust; The haughty Poet's head, the noblest, Bowed on his wounded breast in dust. No longer could his free soul suffer The vulgar world's low infamy; He rose against the world's opinion, And as a hero, lone fell he. He fell! To what avail the sobbing—The useless choir of tears and praise? Wretched the stammering excuses! The Fates have spoke,—no power allays! Have ye not at all times together His sacred genius baited sore, The silent fury fanned to flaming, Delighted in your work before?

"The Sail"

A lone white sail on the horizon Upon the azure sea doth stand. What seeks he in this foreign region? What left he in his native land?

The whistling breeze the mast is bending, The playful waves around him rise. Ah! Not for happiness he searches, And not from happiness he flies.

The sun is bright as gold above him, Light spray below, a snowy fleece; But he, rebellious, seeks the tempest, As though the storms could bring him peace!

"Desires"

Open wide my strong-barred dungeon, Give me sunlight and the day, And a black-browed, black-eyed maiden, And a black-maned steed for play. Let me once across the meadow Gallop on that swift-shod steed, Let me once taste of the madness—Life—and love and all its gladness—That were liberty indeed!

Give me but a wooden dory With half rotted, curving sides, With a gray sail torn to tatters, used to tempests and to tides. Then upon the gray faced ocean In that dory I would leap, All alone, and nothing caring, Wind and tide and tempest daring, I would quarrel with the deep.

Give me then a high built palace, And around it gardens green In whose wide and shady reaches Ripen grapes in amber sheen, And a fountain never silent In the marble palace plays, Muting me, with dew dust hidden, Into pleasant dreams of Eden In the nights and in the days.

CHAPTER FIVE

Alexander Sergeyevitch Pushkin (1799-1837)

* Target of many ugly remarks and biting critics.
* Great-grandfather, who was abducted from modern day Cameroon, was raised in the court of Peter the Great.
* Is to Russian literature what Shakespeare is to Western literature.
* Writings reflect human existence, love, creativeness, and death.
* Sympathetic to anyone fighting against tyranny, violence and oppression of the "human personality".
* Unable to reconcile himself to slavery and arbitrary rule.
* Subject of multiple exiles, severe censorship, slander, humiliation, and denunciations.

"The Queen of Spades"

"Hermann, a Russian military officer, learns that a fellow officer's grandmother, an old countess, possesses the secret of winning at faro, a high-stakes card game. Hermann begins a romantic relationship with the countess's impoverished young ward, to gain access to the old woman. The countess refuses to reveal the secret and dies of fright when Hermann threatens her with a pistol. During the night of her funeral, he dreams that the countess has told him the winning cards—three, seven, and ace. Hermann places bets on the three and seven and wins. After betting everything on the ace, which wins,

Hermann is horror-stricken to see that he is holding not the ace but the queen of spades, who appears to smile up at him as did the countess from her casket."

Passages from "The Queen of Spades"

"..like some misshapen but essential ornament of the ball-room;.."

"The Countess was far from being wicked, but she had the capriciousness of a woman who has been spoiled by the world, and the miserliness and cold-hearted egotism of all old people who have done with loving and whose thoughts lie in the past. She took part in all the vanities of the haut-monde; she dragged herself to balls, where she sat in a corner, rouged and dressed in old-fashioned style, like some misshapen but essential ornament of the ball-room; on arrival, the guests would approach her with low bows, as if in accordance with an established rite, but after that, they would pay no further attention to her."

"..he sighed at the loss imaginary fortune.."

"His imagination was again fired by the amazing story of the three cards. He began to walk around near the house, thinking of its owner and her mysterious faculty. It was late when he returned to his humble rooms; for a long time he could not sleep, and when at last he did drop off, cards, a green table, heaps of banknotes and piles of golden coins appeared to him in his dreams. He played one cards after the other, doubled his stake decisively, won unceasingly, and raked in the golden coins and stuffed his pockets with the banknotes. Waking up late, he sighed at the loss imaginary fortune, again went out to wander about the town."

".. accepting his winnings in the form of promissory notes.."

"There was in Moscow a society of rich gamblers, presided over by the celebrated Chekalinsky, a man whose whole life had been spent at the card-table, and who had amassed millions long ago, accepting his winnings in the form of promissory notes and paying his losses with ready money. His long experience had earned him the confidence of his companions, and his open house, his famous cook and his friendliness and gaiety had won him great public respect. He arrived in Petersburg. The younger generation flocked to his house, forgetting balls for cards, and preferring the enticement of faro to the fascinations of courtship."

"..on the left the one which led to the corridor. Hermann opened the latter,.."

"Two portraits, painted in Paris by Madame Lebrun, hung from one of the walls. One of these featured a plumb, red-faced man of about forty, in a light-green uniform and with a star pinned to his breast; the other—a beautiful young woman with an aquiline nose and powered hair, brushed back at the temples and adorned with a rose. In the corners of the room stood porcelain shepherdesses, table clocks from the workshop of the celebrated Leroy, little boxes, roulettes, fans and the various lady's playthings which had been popular at the end of the last century, when the Montgolfiers' balloon and Mesmer's magnetism were invented. Hermann went behind the door and screen, where stood a small iron bedstead; on the right was the door leading to the study; on the left the one which led to the corridor. Hermann opened the latter, and saw the narrow, winding staircase which led to the poor ward's room…But he turned back and stepped into the dark study."

"The Squire's Daughter"

The story is set in the Russian countryside of the 19th century. The two noble landowners, Muromskiy and Berestov, have been in a quarrel over differing lifestyles and estate management. Muromskiy lives in elegance and adores everything new and foreign. He is fascinated by anything English. He has his own English garden.He demands his daughter talk to him in English and, despite all his debt, hires an English lady as his daughter's governess. His daughter Liza, his only child, is spoiled, vivacious, likes playing pranks, and often gets bored with her calm country life. Berestov, Muromskiy's neighbor, belongs to the conservative class of landowners and rejects any kind of innovations. And he takes every opportunity to mock his too modern neighbor. Berestow has got a son, Alexey, who is eager to serve in the army after his graduation from the university. The young man doesn't fancy his father's provincial style of life. Berestov disapproves of Alexey's decision and demands he comes to the country to live on the estate and become a real Russian landowner.

Passages from "The Squire's Daughter"

"..but her heart beat violently:.."

"In the east the dawn was radiant, and the golden ranks of clouds seemed to be awaiting the sun, like courtiers their sovereign. The clear sky, the morning freshness, the dew, the slight breeze and the singing of the birds filled Lisa's heart with child-like joy. In fear of meeting someone she knew, she seemed not to walk but to fly. As she approached the copse, which formed the boundary to her father's estate, Lisa slowed down. It was here that she was to wait for Alexei. She did not know why but her heart beat violently: it is the excitement that accompanies our youthful pranks which constitutes their principal charm."

"..the departure of a visiting guest leaves behind, sometimes lasting memories."

"Those of my readers who have never lived in the country cannot imagine how charming these young provincial ladies are. Brought up in the open air, beneath the shade of the apple-trees in their gardens, they obtain all their knowledge of life and of the world from books. Solitude, freedom and reading early develop in them feelings and passions unknown to our frivolous townswomen. For these young ladies the jingle of bells is in itself an adventure, a trip to the nearest town a major event in their lives, and the departure of a visiting guest leaves behind, sometimes lasting memories."

".. suddenly found himself not more than a pistol shot away.."

"One fine, cold morning (one of those which so enrich our Russian autumn), Ivan Petrovitch Berestov went out riding, taking with him, in the event of any sport, five or six greyhounds, his whipper-in and a few stable-boys with rattles. At the same time, Grigory Ivanovitch Muromsky, tempted by the fine weather, ordered his bob-tailed filly to be saddled, and himself set out for a gentle trot around his anglicized estate. Approaching the wood, he caught sight of his neighbour, (sic) proudly seated in his saddle, wearing a fox fur-lined jacket, and awaiting the appearance of a hare which his stable-boys, with loud cries and shaking of rattles, were harrying out of a clump of bushes. If Grigory Ivanovitch could have foreseen this encounter, he would have undoubtedly turned in another direction; as it was, however, he came upon Berestov quite unexpectedly and suddenly found himself not more than a pistol shot away from him."

".. almost died of boredom in this barbarous Russia of ours."

"Lisa had not yet seen Alexi; yet among the other young ladies of the neighbourhood (sic) he had become the sole topic of conversation. Lisa was seventeen years old. Her swarthy and attractive face was lit up by dark eyes. She was an only child and consequently very spoilt. Her high spirits and incessant pranks were the delight of her father and the despair of her governess, Miss Jackson, a strait-laced spinster of forty, who powered her face, dyed her eyebrows and read all the way through *Pamela* twice a year—for all of which she received two thousand roubles a year, and almost died of boredom in this barbarous Russia of ours."

∞

"The Blizzard"

In 1811, a seventeen-year-old girl, Maria Gavrilovna, falls in love with a young officer, Vladimir Nikolayevich. Her parents disapprove of the relationship, which continues into the winter through correspondence. Finally they decide to elope, marry quickly, and then throw themselves at the feet of her parents to beg forgiveness.

Maria slipped out in the middle of a winter's night taking a sleigh to a distant village church, where her love would meet her for the wedding. On that night a terrible blizzard was raging, but the girl managed to reach the church as planned. Vladimir, on the other hand, driving alone to the rendezvous, became lost in the dark and the storm, arriving at the church many hours late to find no one there.

Passages from "The Blizzard"

"The storm had still not subsided: I saw a light.."

"…the blizzard had not abated: I grew impatient, again gave orders for the horses to be harnessed, and set out into the teeth of the storm. The driver took it into his head to drive by the river and thus shorten our journey by three versts. The banks of the river were covered with snow; the driver drove past the place where we should have turned off the road, and thus we found ourselves in strange country. The storm had still not subsided: I saw a light and ordered the driver to make for it. We arrived at a village; there was a light in the wooden church. The church was open, and several sledges stood behind the fence; people were walking about inside the porch. 'This way! This way!' Several voices cried."

"… his eyes and his soul followed her."

"Burmin was indeed a most charming young man. He had just the sort of mind that women like; he was decorous, observant without pretensions, and lightly satirical. His behaviour towards Marya Gavrilovna was simple and frank; but whatever she did or said, his eyes and his soul followed her. He seemed to be quiet and modest in character—the rumour had it, however, that he had once been quite a rake, but this did not injure him in the eyes of Marya Gavrilovna, who (like most young ladies) excused with pleasure pranks that indicated a bold or ardent nature."

"... his surroundings disappeared in a thick, yellow fog,.."

"..scarcely had Vladimir left the village behind him and got out into open than the wind blew up and such a blizzard developed that he was unable to see a thing. In one minute the road was hidden; his surroundings disappeared in a thick, yellow fog, through which the white snowflakes swirled; the sky merged with the ground; Vladimir found himself in a field and tried in vain to regain the road; his horse went on at random, repeatedly stepping into a snowdrift or stumbling over a depression in the ground; the sledge was continually overturning. All Vladimir's efforts were concentrated on not losing his way."

"The blizzard had not abated; the wind blew in their faces,.."

"Outside a blizzard raged; the wind howled, and the shutters shook and rattled; everything seemed to her like a threat and a sad omen. Soon all was quiet in the house, and everyone asleep. Masha wrapped a shawl round her head, put on a warm cloak, took her box in her hand, and went out by the back door. Her maid followed her, carrying two bundles. They went into the garden. The blizzard had not abated; the wind blew in their faces, as if striving to stop the young defaulter. They fought their way to the end of the garden. In the road a sledge was waiting for them. The horses, chilled to the marrow, would not keep still."

∽

"The Postmaster"

A poor Russian postmaster is left distraught when his beloved daughter runs away and abandons him for a nobleman.

Upon tracking down his daughter he finds her enjoying a life of wealth and privilege which she is not willing to leave.

Passages from "The Postmaster"

"… came out into the porch (where poor
Dunya has once kissed me),.."

"It was autumn. Grey clouds covered the sky, and a cold wind was blowing across the bare fields, carrying the red and yellow leaves snatched from the trees through which it passed. I arrived in the village at sunset and drew up outside the postmaster's small house. A fat woman came out into the porch (where poor Dunya has once kissed me), and in reply to my questions, stated that the old postmaster had been dead for a year or so, that the house was now occupied by a brewer, and that she was the brewer's wife. I began to regret my useless journey and the seven roubles that I had spent in vain."

"Tear again welled up in his eyes—tears of indignation."

"He stood motionless for a long time; at last he saw that there was a roll of paper beneath the cuff of his sleeve; he drew it out and unfolded several crumpled five-and ten-rouble notes. Tear again welled up in his eyes—tears of indignation. He screwed up the notes into a ball, flung them to the ground, trampled them beneath his heel and went off. After walking a few paces, he stopped and thought …and retracted his steps…but the notes had gone. A well-dressed young man, seeing him, ran up to a carriage, hurriedly got in and shouted to the driver: 'Drive on!'"

"... how he could have allowed his Dunya to go off with the Hussar,.."

"It was a Sunday; Dunya was getting ready to go to mass. The Hussar's sledge was brought around. He said good-bye to the postmaster, rewarding him lavishly for his board and lodging. He also took leave of Dunham offering, as he did so, to drive her as far as the church, which was at the other end of the village. Dunya seemed perplexed.

"What are you frightened of?" Her father asked her. "His Honour is not a wolf; he won't eat you; drive with him as far as the church."

Dunya got into the sledge and sat down beside the Hussar, the servant leaped up onto the coachman's seat, the driver whistled, and the horses galloped off.

The unfortunate postmaster could never understand how he could have allowed his Dunya to go off with the Hussar, how he could have been so blind, what he could have been thinking of. Not half an hour had gone by before his heart began to ache...."

"... postmasters are as a rule peaceful people, obliging by nature,.."

"...over a period of twenty years I have travelled the length and breadth of Russia; almost all the post-roads are known to me; I am acquainted with several generations of drivers; there are few postmasters whom I do not know personally, few with whom I have not had dealings.........postmasters as a whole have been represented to the general public in an extremely false light. These much maligned postmasters are as a rule peaceful people, obliging by nature, sociably inclined, free from exaggerated pretensions about themselves, and not especially fond of money."

CHAPTER SIX

Nikolai Gogol (1809-1852)

* Writing style reflected the grotesque and the absurd to depict shallow worries and pointless cruelty.
* Considered to be one of the "most untranslatable" Russian writers.
* Burned portions of the second part of his popular novel, "Dead Souls" just before he died at age 42.
* An eccentric man with a small physique who loved to travel.
* Interested in the lives of people who built their lives around titles, prestige, and arbitrary notions of superiority.
* Viewed by Tsarist authorities as a literary bridge between Russian and Ukrainian cultures.

"The Overcoat"

Arkaky is a government clerk and copyist in the Russian government who socially fades in the background at home and at work. Although he neglects his appearance, his need to stay warm in the cold of St. Petersburg causes him to replace his current unattractive, thin, tattered, and threadbare coat with a brand new tailored-made overcoat. When his precious new overcoat is stolen no-one seems willing to help him retrieve his prized possession. This continues to concern him even beyond his grave

Passages from "The Overcoat"

"sundry calamities, …are strewn along the path of life,"

"No man could claim having seen him at any evening gathering. Having had his sweet fill of quill-driving, he would lie down to sleep, smiling at the though of the next day: just what would God send him on the morrow?

Such was the peaceful course of life of a man who, with a yearly salary of four hundred, knew how to be content with his lot, and that course might even have continued to a ripe old age had it not been for sundry calamities, such as are strewn along the path of life, not only of titular, but even privy, actual, court, and all other sorts of councilors, even those who never give any counsel to anybody nor ever accept any counsel from others for themselves ."

"…the blizzard that was whistling and howling through the streets;.."

"How he went down the stairs, how he came out into the street—that was something Akakii Akakiievich was no longer conscious of. He felt neither his hands nor his feet; never in all his life had he been dragged over such hot coals by a general—and a general outside his bureau, at that! With his mouth gaping, stumbling off the sidewalk, he breasted the blizzard that was whistling and howling through the streets; the wind, as is its wont in Petersburg, blew upon him from all the four quarters, from every cross lane. In a second it had blown a quinsy down his throat, and he crawled home without the strength to utter a word; he became all swollen and took to his bed."

"… that alcoholic odor which makes the eyes smart…"

"As he clambered up the staircase that led to Petrovich—-the staircase, to render it its just due, was dripping all over from water and slops and thoroughly permeated with that alcoholic odor which makes the eyes smart and is, as everyone knows, unfailingly present on all the backstairs of all the houses in Petersburg— as he clambered up this staircase Akakii Akakiievich was already conjecturing how stiff Petrovich's asking price would be and mentally determined not to give him more than two rubles. The door was open, because the mistress of the place, being busy preparing some fish, had filled the kitchen with so much smoke that one actually couldn't see the very cockroaches for it."

"… feel their foreheads aching because of the frost and the tears come to their eyes,."

"There is, in Petersburg, a formidable foe of all those whose salary runs to four hundred a year or thereabouts. This foe is none other than our northern frost—even though, by the bye, they do say that it's the most healthful thing for you. At nine in the morning, precisely at that hour when the streets are thronged with those on their way to sundry bureaus, it begins dealing out such powerful and penetrating fillips to all noses, without any discrimination, that the poor bureaucrats absolutely do not know how to hide them. At this time, when even those who fill the higher posts feel their foreheads aching because of the frost and the tears come to their eyes, the poor titular councilors are sometimes utterly defenseless. The sole salvation, if one's overcoat is the thinnest, lies in dashing, as quickly as possible, through five or six blocks and then stamping one's feet for a long time in the porter's room, until the faculties and gifts for administrative duties, which have been frozen on the way, are thawed out at last."

∽

"St. John's Eve"

How far will a man go for love? This short story recounts the sinister events that transpired in a poor hamlet generations ago. A young man called Petro falls head over heels for a beauty woman. Determined to win the hand of the woman of his choosing, Petro solicits an ominous local, who is rumored to be the devil incarnate, to help him. The consequences of this assistance are wicked, dangerous and cannot be reversed.

Passages from "St. John's Eve"

"... young women in tall headdresses, the upper part made all of gold brocade,.."

"Weddings in the old days were no comparison with ours. My grandfather's aunt used to tell us—oh, ho, ho! How girls in festive headdresses of yellow, blue, and pink stripes trimmed with gold braids, in fine shirts stitched with red silk and embroidered with little silver flowers, in Morocco boos with high, iron-shod heels, capered about the room as smoothly as peahens and swishing like the wind; how young women in tall headdresses, the upper part made all of gold brocade, with a small cutout behind and a golden kerchief peeking from it, with two little peaks of the finest black astrakhan, one pointing backward and the other forward, in blue jackets of the best silk with red flaps, stepped out imposingly one by one, arms akimbo, and rhythmically stamped away at the gopak."

"… his mind darkened… As if insane, he seized the knife and innocent blood spurted into his eyes…"

"The witch stamped her foot: blue flame burst from the ground; its whole inside lit up and looked as if it were molded from crystal; and everything under the ground became visible as in the palm of your hand. Gold coins, precious stones, in chests, in cauldrons, were heaped up right under the place where they stood. His eyes glowed… his mind darkened… As if insane, he seized the knife and innocent blood spurted into his eyes… A devilish guffawing thundered on all sides. Hideous monsters leaped before him in throngs. The witch, clutching the beheaded corpse, drank its blood like a wolf… Everything whirled in his head! Summoning all his strength, he broke into a run. Everything before him was covered with red. The trees, bathed in blood, seemed to burn and groan. The sky, red hot, was trembling… Fiery spots, like lightning came to his eyes. Exhausted, he ran inside his hut and collapsed as if he had been mowed down. A dead sleep came over him."

"… lightning flashed in the sky and a whole bank of flowers appeared before him,…"

"He approached the the knolls: Where are the flowers? Nothing could be seen. Wild weeds stood blackly around, stifling everything with their thickness. But now lightning flashed in the sky and a whole bank of flowers appeared before him, all wondrous, all never seen before; there were also simple ferns. Doubt came over Petro, and he stood before them pondering, arms akimbo."

"... the branches of the trees were decked with hoarfrost as if with hare's fur."

"Many Cossacks had reaped their hay, and harvested their crops, many Cossacks, the more riotous sort, had set out on campaign. Flocks of ducks still crowed our marshes, but the bitterns were long gone. The steppes were turning red. Shocks of wheat stood here and there like bright Cossack hats strewn over the fields. On the road you would meet carts piled with kindling and firewood. The ground turned harder and in places was gripped by frost. Snow had already begun to spatter from the sky, and the branches of the trees were decked with hoarfrost as if with hare's fur. On a clear, frosty day, the red-breasted bullfinch, like a foppish Polish gentleman, was already strolling over the snowdrifts pecking at seeds, and children with enormous sticks were sending wooden whirligigs over the ice, while their fathers calmly stayed stretched on the stove, stepping out every once in a while, a lighted pipe in their teeth, to say a word or two about the good Orthodox frost, or to get some fresh air and thresh some grain that had long been sitting in the front hall."

ↄﬗ

"Old World Landowners"

A solitary elderly couple, Afanasy Ivanovich and his wife Pulkheria, live by themselves in a remote village. They are good-hearted, childless, and very tender to each other. They oversee and ineffectively manage a farm on which many serf girls and stewards do most of the laborious jobs. In addition to eating many meals throughout the day, Afanasy likes to tease his wife. He "pokes fun at her" by wanting to know what they would do if their house burned down. When Afanasy wants a mid-morning meal, Pulkheria whips out poppy-seed hand pies, pickled mushrooms, and a silver goblet of vodka at ten in the morning.

But what happens if one of them dies, leaving the other completely alone?

Passages from "Old World Landowners"

"… however much the steward and headman stole, however much everyone in the household stuffed his face,.."

"Those worthy rulers, the steward and the headman, thought it quite unnecessary to bring all the flour into the master's own barn and that half was enough; in the end, even the half that was delivered was either moldy or damp and had been rejected at the fair. But however much the steward and headman stole, however much everyone in the household stuffed his face, from the housekeeper to the pigs, who consumed a terrible quantity of plums and apples, and often shoved the trees with their snouts to shake down a whole rain of fruit; however much the sparrows and crows pecked up; however much all the household people took as presents to their kin in other villages, even stealing old linen and yard from the storerooms, all of which returned to the universal source, that is, the tavern; however much visitors, their phlegmatic coachmen and lackeys stole— the blessed earth produced everything in such abundance….that all this terrible plundering seemed to go entirely unnoticed …"

"... often in childhood: sometimes my name would suddenly be distinctly spoken behind me."

"It has undoubtedly happened to you that you hear a voice calling you by name, something simple people explain by saying that a soul is longing for the person and calling him, and after that comes inevitable death…..I remember hearing it often in childhood: sometimes my name would suddenly be distinctly spoken behind me. Usually, at the moment, it was a most clear and sunny day; not a leaf stirred on any tree in the garden, there was a dead silence, even the grasshoppers would stop chirring at that moment; not a soul in the garden; yet I confess that if night, most furious and stormy, with all the inferno of the elements, had overtaken me alone amid an impenetrable forest, I would not have been as frightened of it as of this terrible silence amid a cloudless day."

"I like sometimes to descend…into the realm of this remarkably solitary life,…"

"I like very much the modest life of those solitary proprietors of remote estates who in Little Russia are usually known as the old world and who, like decrepit, picturesque little houses, are so the nicely mottled and so completely the opposite of a new, smooth building whose walls have not yet been washed by rain, whose roof is not yet covered with green mold, and whose porch does not yet show its red bricks through missing plaster. I like sometimes to descend for a moment into the realm of this remarkably solitary life, where not one desire flies over the paling that surrounds the small yard, over the wattle fence that encloses the garden filled with apples and plum trees, over the village cottages surrounding it, slumping to one side, in the shade of pussy willows, elders, and pear trees."

"… everything we are parted from is dear to us."

"…in front of the house, a vast yard of low, fresh grass, with a beaten path from the barn to the kitchen and from the kitchen to the master's quarters; a long-necked goose drinking water with her young, downy-soft goslings; the paling hung with strings of dried pears and apples and rugs airing out; a cart full of melons standing by the barn; an unharnessed ox lying lazily beside it—all this has an inexplicable charm for me, perhaps because I no longer see it, and because everything we are parted from is dear to us. Be that as it may, even as my britzka drove up to the porch of this little house, my soul would assume a remarkably pleasant and calm state;.."

⌒⌒

"The Carriage"

An action takes place in a town that is terribly boring, and the streets are deserted. Once the cavalry regiment comes in this town everything changes immediately. The town comes alive and takes a completely different view. In addition, a general comes here who likes to arrange dinner parties, and there are always a lot of people at these parties (mainly consisting of military officers and some landowners). The most famous landowner once served in one of the cavalry regiments. Now retired he does not miss any opportunity to visit with the officers. During a dinner party the landowner invites the local military general and his entourage to his house the next day to see a carriage which he hope to sell the general for a handsome profit. Things, however, do not quite work out as planned.

Passages from "The Carriage"

"... dust suddenly rising in the distance caught her attention."

"...she went on sitting in the dense alley, from which a view opened onto the high road, and gazing absentmindedly at its unpeopled emptiness, when dust suddenly rising in the distance caught her attention. Looking closer, she soon made out several carriages. At their head drove a light, open two-seater; in it sat the general, his thick epaulettes gleaming in the sun, with the colonel beside him. It was followed by another, a four-seater; in it sat the major, with the general's aide-de-camp and two officers on the facing seats; ..."

"... it's impossible to describe what would come over your heart...such anguish..."

"The little town of B. became much gayer when the——-cavalry regiment was stationed there. Before then, it was awfully boring. When you happened to drive through it and gaze at the low cob houses looking out so incredibly sourly, it's impossible to describe what would come over your heart then—such anguish as if you'd lost at cards or blurted out something stupid at the wrong time; in short, no good. The cob has fallen off of them on account of the rain, and the walls, instead of white, have become piebald;..."

"... soldiers with mustaches as stiff as a bootblack's brush."

"The wooden fences between houses were all dotted with soldiers' caps hanging out in the sun; a gray overcoat was bound to be sticking up somewhere on a gate; in the lanes you might run into soldiers with mustaches as stiff as a bootblack's brush.

These mustaches could be seen in all places. If tradeswomen got together at the market with their dippers, a mustache was sure to be peeking over their shoulders. In the middle of the square, a soldier with a mustache was sure to be soaping the beard of some village yokel, who merely grunted, rolling up his eyes."

"…everything was in harmony with everything else."

"….the beautiful summer day, the windows all thrown wide open, the plates of ice on the table, the gentlemen officers with their bottom button unbuttoned, the owners of trim tailcoats with their shirt fronts all rumpled, the crisscross conversation dominated by the general's voice and drowned in champagne—-everything was in harmony with everything else."

∾

"The Portrait"

A young artist buys a mysterious portrait in a downtown Saint Petersburg shop. The eyes of the portrait seem to be alive, they have an evil stare. That night the portrait comes to life and the stranger steps out of the frame and starts counting money on the bed in front of the terrified artist. Lots of money. The next day the frame breaks accidentally revealing a large amount of golden coins hidden in the frame.

Passages from "The Portrait"

"... his brush had served as a tool of the devil,..."

"This story made a strong impression on my father. He fell to pondering seriously, lapsed into hypochondria, and in the end became fully convinced that his brush had served as a tool of the devil, that part of the moneylender's life had indeed passed somehow into the portrait and was now troubling people, inspiring them with demonic impulses, seducing the artist from his path, generating terrible torments of envy...."

"Most extraordinary of all were the eyes:.."

"..the artist had already been standing motionless for some time before a portrait in a big, once magnificent frame, on which traces of gilding now barely gleamed. It was an old man with a face the color of bronze, gaunt, high-cheekboned; the features seemed to have been caught at a moment of convulsive movement and bespoke an un-northern force. Fiery noon was stamped on them. He was draped in a loose Asiatic costume. Damaged and dusty though the portrait was, when he managed to clean the dust off the face, he could see the marks of a lofty artist's work. The portrait, it seemed, was unfinished; but the force of the brush was striking. Most extraordinary of all were the eyes:…"

"Light, half-transparent shadows fell
tail-like on the ground,.."

"… he walked on almost mechanically, with hurried steps, insensible to everything. The red light of the evening sun still lingered over half the sky; the houses turned toward it still glowed faintly with its warm light; and meanwhile the cold, bluish radiance of the moon grew stronger. Light, half-transparent shadows fell tail-like on the ground, cast by houses and the legs of passers-by. The artist was beginning gradually to admire the sky, aglow with some transparent, thin, uncertain light and almost simultaneously the words "What a light tone!" and "It's irksome, devil take it!" flew out of his mouth. And, straightening the portrait, which kept slipping from under his arm, he quickened his pace."

"... no longer art: it even destroyed the harmony of the portrait..."

"But here, in the portrait now before him, there was nevertheless something strange. This was no longer art: it even destroyed the harmony of the portrait itself. They were alive, they were human eyes! It seemed as if they had been cut out of a living man and set there. Here there was not that lofty pleasure which comes over the soul at the sight of an artist's work, however terrible its chosen subject; here there was some morbid, anguished feeling. "What is it?" the artist asked himself involuntarily. "It's nature all the same, it's living nature—why, then, this strangely unpleasant feeling?"

CHAPTER SEVEN

Maxim Gorky(1868-1936)

* Born into the impoverished lower depths of Russian society.
* Left home at the age of twelve and taught himself to read while working various backbreaking jobs.
* Imprisoned for writing a proclamation inspired by a student demonstration that was brutally suppressed by government authorities .
* Described by Anton Chekhov as, "a destroyer bound to destroy everything that deserved destruction."
* Early writings describe the life of simple people who were victims of the 1891-92 famine.

"My Fellow-Traveller- A Journey" (A Sophisticated Traveller)

This is a novella by and about the author Maxim Gorky who meets a stranger at the harbor of the city of Odessa. After listening to the stranger's sad story, Gorky decides to help him and sets on a long journey in which he gets through many interesting and dangerous adventures. This is a story of that journey and those adventures.

Passages from "My Fellow-Traveller"

"Fires appear to cause peculiar gratification to all men,.."

"I've noticed that people usually have a kind of idolatrous passion for fire… All high festivities, royal anniversaries, birthdays, marriages and other little motives of human rejoicings- excepting funerals- are accompanied by fireworks and illuminations. Divine services, too - but there one must also include funerals. Small urchins amuse themselves by lighting wood-piles even in summer time - for which they ought to be unmercifully spanked, as these pranks are usually the case of forest fires. Fires appear to cause peculiar gratification to all men, and everybody rushes at them like moths. A poor man is pleased to see a rich man's house burning; in fact every person endowed with organs for seeing is attracted by fire -…"

"… soldierly face is lit by a pair of clear eyes.."

"Vinokuroff is more than fifty, but he is still a strong, sturdy man. His wood-cut, soldierly face is lit by a pair of clear eyes that look at you calmly, with the look of a man who has seen a lot, who has lost the habit of being astonished at anything and is a stranger to all anxieties. He looks somehow across people, not straight at them, and treats them with a certain amount of condescension."

"For an idler life is just one long boredom."

"A man on board ship acquires a funny childishness, apart from the fact that almost everybody is humiliatingly sea-sick. And at sea one notices, more acutely than one does on shore, what a non-entity man is. In this fact lies the moral which sea voyages teach us. To cut it short, I can safely assert that on the whole surface of the globe, land or water, there is nothing worse than passengers. For an idler life is just one long boredom. Well, at sea boredom is especially poisonous, and all passengers are by nature idle people. Out of sheer boredom they lose their personalities to such an extent that in spite of high titles, decorations, riches and other distinctions, they treat simple firemen as equals. Like dogs at the sight of oatmeal biscuits, they rush to the deck to enjoy the view of a foreign shore."

"...unused to seeing blood flow freely."

"Yet I have seen numberless cases of our own Russian men, sailors, workmen and others, being torn to pieces, smashed, bruised under my eyes, without this affecting the passengers in the slightest, unless one counts the natural anxiety and nervous perturbation that occur when one is unused to seeing blood flow freely."

༄

"Peculiar Tramp"

This is the story of a man who is sitting around frightening laborers with stories, advice, and lectures about devils. What makes this man particularly special is his is one of a number of wealthy Russian noblemen who become professional tramps during certain times of the year, but return to their normal lifestyle when the occasion suits them.

Passages from "Peculiar Tramp"

"… the shoes on his feet showed that he was earning a decent living."

"His fine baritone rang out gaily, and the words rolled lightly from his tongue. His thick linen military shirt, his wide Turkish trousers and the shoes on his feet showed that he was earning a decent living. I reminded him where I had first seen him; and he listened to me attentively, picking his teeth with a stem of grass."

"He sat as though he was about to spring across the table."

"The guest raised his head and lowered it again, leaning his chin on the edge of the table, so that he looked as though he had been decapitated. He sat in a crouching attitude, his chair pushed as far away as possible from the table, and his hands hidden under the cloth. From both sides of a bald head shocks of grayish hair stuck out in a provoking way, like horns, disclosing two small ears. The lobes of his ears had a very definite contour. And seemed to be swollen. His chin was clean-shaven, but a grey mustache protruded from under his nose, giving him a martial appearance. He wore a blue shirt. His collar, torn and unbuttoned, exposed to view portions of an unwashed neck and a muscular right shoulder. He sat as though he was about to spring across the table."

"… on a heap of stones sat a man dressed in a light cotton summer suit,…"

"On the high road, over the Laba, a group of Rostoff tramps were breaking road-metal. I came across them at night, when their day's work was ended and they were getting ready to have some tea. A fat tramp with a long grey beard was busy boiling the kettle over a small wood-fire; three of his comrades were resting among the shrubs at the side of the road, while on a heap of stones sat a man dressed in a light cotton summer suit, and wearing a wide-brimmed straw hat and white shoes. He was holding a cigarette between his fingers, and as he slashed the grey, thin smoke of the tobacco with a cane, he talked to those around him, without troubling to glance in their direction."

"The heavy silence of an autumn night pervaded the atmosphere,.."

"In the golden glow of the burning logs purple tongues danced about and blue flowers blossomed. A luminous vault hung in the darkness over the fire. We sat under a shining dome, enclosed and oppressed by the surrounding blackness. The heavy silence of an autumn night pervaded the atmosphere, and in the failing light the broken fragments of rock might have been wisps of mist, frozen into solidity."

∽

"The Outcasts"

A group of men degraded, ragged, angry, filthy, broken-down by life, and saturated with vodka are engaged in heated, sometimes violent, disputes on subjects such as "the necessity of conquering India", "sweeping the Jews off the face of the earth", and rendering derogatory commits about women. These are the outcasts.

Passages from "Outcasts"

"…dilapidated roofs, disfigured by time, patched with shingles,.."

"The high street consists of two rows of one-storeyed hovels, squeezed close one against another; old hovels with leaning walls and crooked windows, with dilapidated roofs, disfigured by time, patched with shingles, and overgrown with moss; here and there above them rise tall poles surmounted with starling houses, whilst the roofs are shaded by the dusty green of pollard willows and elder bushes, the sole miserable vegetation of suburbs where dwell the poorest classes."

"…a mouthful of pure water does not satisfy a hungry stomach."

"Thus, in dull anger, in trouble that crushed the heart, in the uncertainty of the issue of this miserable existence, they spent the autumn days awaiting the still harder days of winter. During hard times like these Kouvalda would come to their rescue with his philosophy. 'Pluck up courage, lads! All comes to an end! — that's what there is best about life! Winter will pass and summer will follow; good times when, as they say, "even a sparrow has beer"! But his speeches were of little avail; a mouthful of pure water does not satisfy a hungry stomach."

"At intervals the silence was broken by….."

"It was quiet enough; in the cloud-covered sky, which threatened rain, and on the earth, shrouded in the still silence of an autumn night. At intervals the silence was broken by the snoring of those who had fallen asleep; by the gurgle of vodka being poured from the bottle, or the noisy munching of food. The deacon was muttering something. The clouds hung so low that it almost seemed as if they would catch the roof of the old house, and overturn it on to the outcasts."

"He seemed to be quietly and peacefully smiling,.."

"The cart moved off, jolting along the uneven surface of the yard. The schoolmaster's body covered with some scanty rags, and lying face upwards, shook and tumbled about with the jolting of the cart. He seemed to be quietly and peacefully smiling, as if pleased with the though that he was leaving the doss-house, never to return— never any more."

"...all that soiled this sad, miserable, tortured earth."

"The threatening sky looked down quietly at the dirty yard, and the trim little old man with the sharp grey beard, who walked about measuring and calculating with his cunning eyes. On the roof of the old house sat a crow triumphantly croaking, and swaying backwards and forwards with outstretched neck. The grey lowering clouds, with which the whole sky was covered, seemed fraught with suspense and inexorable design, as if ready to burst and pour forth torrents of water, to wash away all that soiled this sad, miserable, tortured earth."

∽

"On The Steppes"

While traveling together along a lonely road, three unemployed men, united by life's misfortunes, see a stranger lying on the ground. As they approach, the stranger threatens them with a pistol. Suddenly a shot is fired and the situation quickly went from bad to worst.

Passages from "On The Steppes"

"It smouldered gently in the quiet windless night,.."

"We went off to fetch the fuel which we had left at the place where we had been arrested by the shout of the cabinetmaker. We collected it again, and were soon sitting round a comfortable fire. It smouldered gently in the quiet windless night, and lit up the spot on which we were seated. We were getting sleepy, but we could still have eaten another supper."

"He hated both town and village with the hatred of an impotent hunted hungry animal,.."

"The second one of the party was a shriveled, dried up little man, with thin lips, always skeptically pursed up; and when he told us that he was a former student of Moscow University, the soldier and I took it as a matter of course. As a matter of fact it was all the same to us whether he was a student, a spy, or a rogue. All that concerned us was that during our present acquaintanceship he was our equal; he was hungry, he enjoyed in towns the special attention of the police, and in villages was looked upon by the peasants with suspicion. He hated both town and village with the hatred of an impotent hunted hungry animal, and used to dream of a general vengeance on all and on everything. In a word, as regards his position amongst the chosen ones of nature, and the powerful ones of life, and as regards his disposition, he was one of us."

"... looking like a huge round flat black bowl, under the hot blue dome.."

"We, trudged along… and on all sides of us stretched the immense boundless steppes, looking like a huge round flat black bowl, under the hot blue dome of a summer sky. The grey, dusty road cut through the distance like a broad stripe, whilst its baked surface burnt our feet. From time to time we came across bristly patches of freshly cut corn, which bore a strange resemblance to the soldier's stubbly cheeks. He stepped along, singing in a rather hoarse voice."

> *"we tramped along the vast and silent steppes*
> *in the ruddy rays of the sunset,."*

"Striving thus to shallow down the saliva of hunger, and making an effort to appease the tortures of the stomach by friendly talk, we tramped along the vast and silent steppes in the ruddy rays of the sunset,… full of vague hope … We watched the sun sinking quietly into the soft clouds, richly coloured by its rays, whilst behind us, and on either side, a bluish mist rising up from the steppes towards the sky veiled the gloomy landscape behind us."

♒

"Twenty-Six and One"

In a factory, located in a building that contains an embroidery shop where a young chambermaid lives and work, twenty-six men work from morning to night making biscuits, cakes, and bread. Every morning the factory workers give the girl fresh biscuits and bread. This cordiality ends when a new worker, a self-proclaimed womanizer, comes to the factory.

Passages from "Twenty-Six and One"

"... we all went back silently to our damp, stony ditch."

"We remained standing in the centre of the yard, in the mud, under the rain and the grey, sunless sky…. Then we all went back silently to our damp, stony ditch. As before, the sun never peeped in through our windows, and Tanya never came there again!…"

"... twenty-six living machines, locked up in a damp cellar,.."

"There were twenty-six of us— twenty-six living machines, locked up in a damp cellar, where we patted dough from morning till night, making biscuits and cakes. The windows from our cellar looked out into a ditch, which was covered with bricks grown green from dampness, the window frames were obstructed from the outside by a dense iron netting, and the light of the sun could not peep in through the panes, which were covered with flour-dust."

"... his big, light eyes looked good — kind and clear."

"The cold air, forcing itself in at the door in a thick, smoky cloud, was whirling around his feet; he stood on the threshold, looking down on us from above, and from under his fair, curled mustache, big, yellow teeth were flashing. His waistcoat was blue, embroidered with flowers; it was beaming, and the buttons were of some red stones. And there was a chain too. He was handsome, this soldier, tall, strong, with red cheeks, and his big, light eyes looked good — kind and clear. On his head was a white, stiffly-starched cap, and from under his clean apron peeped out sharp toes of stylish, brightly shining boots."

"… caressing tune always gives ease to the troubled soul.."

"During work someone would suddenly heave a sigh, like that of a tired horse, and would softly start one of those drawling songs, whose touchingly caressing tune always gives ease to the troubled soul of the singer. One of us sang, and at first we listened in silence to his lonely song, which was drowned and deafened underneath the heavy ceiling of the cellar, like the small fire of a wood-pile in the steppe on a damp autumn night, when the grey sky is hanging over the earth like a leaden roof."

❧

CHAPTER EIGHT

Anton Chekhov(1860-1904)

* Writings focused on the everyday texture of life of people filled with the feeling of hopelessness and fruitlessness.
* Better known for his dramatic rather than fictional works.
* Criticized for dealing with serious social and moral questions without furnishing answers.
* Strived to be a dispassionate, non-judgmental author providing truthful descriptions of persons and objects.
* Maxim Gorky noted that, "After reading even Chekhov's most insignificant story everything else seems crude, written not with a pen, but a log."

"The Pipe"

While walking through the wood with his dog, a hunter encounters an old shepherd playing a pipe. The strange melody being played by the shepherd "seem to weep" and reenforce the hunter's pessimistic outlook regarding the world, life, and mankind.

Passages from "The Pipe"

"… felt insufferably sorry for the sky and the earth.."

"Meliton plodded along to the river, and heard the sounds of the pipe gradually dying away behind him. He still wanted to complain. He looked dejectedly about him, and felt insufferably sorry for the sky and the earth and the sun and the woods and his Damka, and when the highest drawn-out note of the pipe floated quivering in the air, like a voice weeping, he felt extremely bitter and resentful of the impropriety in the conduct of nature. The high note quivered, broke off, and the pipe was silent."

"… the sound floated from it uncertainly, with no regularity,.."

"Driving his herd together to the edge of the wood, the shepherd leaned against the birch-tree, looked up at the sky, without haste took his pipe from his bosom and began playing. As before, he played mechanically and took no more than five or six notes, as though the pipe had come into his hands for the first time, the sound floated from it uncertainly, with no regularity, not blending into a tune, but to Meliton, brooding the destruction of the world, there was a sound in it of something very depressing and revolting which he would much rather not have heard."

"It's all going the same way…. There is nothing good to be looked for."

"The shepard looked at the sky, from which a drizzling rain was falling, at the wood, at the bailiff's wet clothes, pondered and said nothing. 'The whole summer has been the same," sighed Meliton. "A bad business for the peasants and no pleasure for the gentry." The shepherd looked at the sky again, thought a moment, and said deliberately, as though chewing each word: "It's all going the same way…. There is nothing good to be looked for.""

> *"What's the good of cleverness to a*
> *huntsman if there is no game?.."*

"What earthly good is cleverness to people on the brink of ruin? One can perish without cleverness. What's the good of cleverness to a huntsman if there is no game? What I think is that God has given men brains and taken away their strength. People have grown weak, exceedingly weak....... I am the humblest peasant in the whole village, and yet, young man, I have strength. Mind you, I am in my seventies, and I tend my herd day in and day out, and I keep the night watch, too, for twenty kopecks, and I don't sleep, and I don't feel the cold; my son is cleverer than I am, but put him in my place and he would ask for a rise next day, or would be going to the doctors."

∽

"The Grasshopper"

A young socialite makes a special effort to befriend stars of the artistic, literary, and dramatic worlds. She is praised for the variety of her talents—sketching, singing, playing musical instruments, and acting—but has never become expert at any one skill. She meets, falls in love, and marries the young doctor who was attending the deathbed of her ailing father. Although she was attracted to her husband's unselfishness, she found him to be a rather ordinary and boring person. Eventually she viewed his simplicity, common sense, and good nature as a sign of weakness and has an adulterous affair with a local artist.

Passages from "The Grasshopper"

"... unable to believe that he would never wake again."

"She wanted to explain to him that it had been a mistake, that all was not lost, that life might still be beautiful and happy, that he was an extraordinary, rare, great man, and that she would all her life worship him and bow down in homage and holy awe before him ... "Dymov!" She called him, patting him on the shoulder, unable to believe that he would never wake again. "Dymov! Dymov!""

"... to sink into forgetfulness., to die, to become a memory.."

"On a still moonlight night in July Olga Ivanovna was standing on the deck of the Volga steamer and looking alternately at the water and at the picturesque banks. Beside her was standing Ryabovsky, telling her the black shadows on the water were not shadows, but a dream, that it would be sweet to sink into forgetfulness., to die, to become a memory in the sight of that enchanted water with the fantastic glimmer, in sight of the fathomless sky and the mournful, dreamy shores that told of the vanity of our life and of the existence of something higher, blessed, and eternal."

"but you have one serious defect. You take absolutely no interest in art..."

"Between four and five she dined at home with her husband. His simplicity, good sense, and kindheartedness touched her and moved her up to enthusiasm. She was constantly jumping up, impulsively hugging his head and showering kisses on it. "You are a clever, generous man, Dymov," she used to say, "but you have one serious defect. You take absolutely no interest in art. You don't believe in music or painting." "I don't understand them," he would say mildly. "I have spent all my life in working at natural science and medicine, and I have never had time to take an interest in the arts.""

"… spring was at hand, already smiling in the distance,."

"…. life flowed on peaceful and happy, free from grief and anxiety. The present was happy, and to follow it spring was at hand, already smiling in the distance, and promising a thousand delights. There would be no end to their happiness; in April, May and June a summer villa a good distance out of town; walks, sketching, fishing, nightingales; and then from July right on to autumn an artist's tour on the Volga, and in this tour Olga Ivanovna would take part as an indispensable member of the society."

♋

"Gooseberries"

The sky is overcast with heavy clouds as two older men walk across the fields, but no rain. As one of the men prepares to tell his friend a story and lights his pipe in preparation a storm breaks and the men run to shelter at their friend's nearby estate.

Passages from "Gooseberries"

"It was damp, muddy, and desolate; the water looked cold and malignant."

"The watermill was at work, drowning the sound of the rain, the dam was shaking. Here wet horses with drooping heads were standing near their carts, and men were walking about covered with sacks. It was damp, muddy, and desolate; the water looked cold and malignant. Ivan Ivanovitch and Burkin were already conscious of a feeling of wetness, messiness, and discomfort all over, their feet were heavy with mud, and when, crossing the dam, they went up to the barns, they were silent, as though they were angry with one another."

"There is no happiness, and there ought not to be;.."

"… he said in an imploring voice, "don't be calm and contented, don't let yourself be put to sleep! While you are young, strong, confident, be not weary in well-doing! There is no happiness, and there ought not to be; but if there is a meaning and an object in life, that meaning and object is not our happiness, but something greater and more rational. Do good!"

"… it was still day, not hot, but heavy,…"

"The whole sky had been overcast with rain-clouds from early morning; it was still day, not hot, but heavy, as it is in grey dull weather when the clouds have been hanging over the country. Ivan Ivanovitch, the veterinary surgeon, and Burkin, the high-school teacher, were already tired from walking, and the fields seemed to them endless."

"… it's monasticism of a sort, but monasticism without good works."

"To retreat from town, from the struggle, from the bustle of life, to retreat and bury oneself in one's farm—-it's not life, it's egoism, laziness, it's monasticism of a sort, but monasticism without good works. A man does not need six feet of earth or a farm, but the whole globe, all nature, where he can have room to display all the qualities and peculiarities of his free spirit."

✍

"In the Ravine"

Ukleevo is a grimy, nondescript village contaminated by pollutants from its three calico factories and inhabited by discontented peasants. Located in a ravine it is renowned because an old sexton had gorged himself on caviar at one of the factory owner's funerals ten years before the story begins. Grigori Tsybukin, with the aid of his wife, two son, and a daughter, runs the local grocery store but supplements his income by selling home-brewed vodka on the sly.

The Tsybukin family, described as one of greed and split loyalties, find themselves embroiled in village feuds and sinister ambitions.

Passages from "In the Ravine

"In the darkness she could see the outliners of two carts,.."

"By the wayside a camp fire was burning ahead of her; the flames had died down, there were only red embers. She could hear the horses munching. In the darkness she could see the outliners of two carts, one with a barrel, the other, a lower one with sacks in it, and the figures of two men; one leading a horse to put it into the shafts, the other was standing motionless by the fire with his hands behind his back. A dog growled by the carts. The one who was leading the horse stopped and said:…"

"... the refuse contaminated the meadows, the peasants' cattle suffered from..."

"The three cotton factories and the tanyard were not in the village itself but a little way off. They were small factories, and not more than four hundred workmen were employed in all of them. The tanyard often made the water in the little river stink; the refuse contaminated the meadows, the peasants' cattle suffered from Siberian plague, and orders were given that the factory should be closed. It was considered to be closed, but went on working in secret with the connivance of the local police officer and the district doctor, who was paid ten roubles a month by the owner."

"Passersby bow to him, but he does not respond,..."

"For some reason, summer and winter alike, he wears a fur coat, and only in very hot weather he does not go out but sits at home. As a rule putting on his fur coat, wrapping it round him and turning up his collar, he walks about the village, along the road to the station, or sits from morning till night on the seat near the church gates. He sits there without stirring. Passersby bow to him, but he does not respond, for as of old he dislikes the peasants. If he is asked a question he answers quite rationally and politely, but briefly."

"... their noses and their cheeks.... were covered with red brick-dust."

"The village was already plunged in the dusk of evening and the sun only gleamed on the upper part of the road which ran wriggling like a snake up the slope. Old women were coming back from the woods and children with them; they were bringing baskets of mushrooms. Peasant women and girls came in a crowd from the station where they had been loading the trucks with bricks, and their noses and their cheeks under their eyes were covered with red brick-dust. They were singing."

✏

"Excerpts From Personal Letters"

Anton Chekhov wrote thousands of letters over his life. Their subjects included: business matters, messages to his wife, family members and close friends, intensely personal matters, and literary observations and insights.

Undated letter [1900]

"...... We are leading a provincial life, the streets of our city are not even paved, our villages are poor, and our people are worn out. In our youth, we twitter like a bunch of sparrows on a pile of manure. At forth we are already old and starting to think about death. What sort of heroes are we?... I only wanted to tell people honestly: look, look how badly you live, how boring your lives are. The important thing is that people should understand this; if they do understand this, they will certainly invent a different and a far better life. Man will become better only once we have shown him as he really is."

Letter to Maxim Gorky, Yalta, February 9, 1900

"You need to see more, know more, and broaden the scope of what you now. You have an imagination with a long reach and a powerful grasp, but it is like a big oven that never gets enough kindling. This comes across in all your work, but especially so in your stories. You've got two or three characters in your story, but they stand apart from the rest of the crowd.

What is obvious is that these characters —-and only these characters —-have come alive in your imagination, while the crowd somehow remains untouched…..."

Letter to Alexander Zhirkevich, Melikhovo, April 2, 1895

"The story should begin with the sentence, "Somov, it seems, was upset." Everything that comes before——-that stuff about the cloud prostrating itself, about the sparrows, the field stretching out into the distance—-all these elements are just so much tribute paid to routine. You do have a feeling for nature, but you do not describe it the way you feel it. Descriptions of nature should first of all be visual, so that when the reader closes his eyes, he can immediately imagine the landscape that was just described;…."

Letter to Yakov Polonsky, Moscow, January 18, 1888

"By the way, I am just now at work on a long story that will probably appear in the *Northern Herald*. In my novella, I describe the steppe, the people of the steppe, the birds, the nights, storms, etc. I'm enjoying the work, but I do worry that because I lack experience in writing long pieces my tone might be inconsistent, I grow tired, I don't say everything that needs to be said, and I am not being serious enough…….."

CHAPTER NINE

Leo Tolstoy(1828-1910)

✱ Writings which are full of long sentences and scrupulous details paint a world in which extreme things happen to ordinary people.

✱ A pacifist, advocate of non-violent resistance who was an opponent of the Russian state system.

✱ Works emphasized the ways in which people related to one another in a societal context.

✱ Spent the latter part of his life exploring the question, "If God does not exist, since death is inevitable, what is the meaning of life?"

✱ Opined that the meaning of life and universal happiness is kindness.

✱ Much of his writings taught morality through vivid images, epithets, metaphors, humor, metonymy, and sarcasm.

"The Sebastopol Sketches"

The story is set in Sevastopol, a city in Crimea, and takes place during the Crimean war. The story is told in three parts: "Sevastopol in December", "Sevastopol in May", and "Sevastopol in August". In the December tale the narrative provides a detailed tour of the city. In the May the narrator examines and muses about the senselessness of war. In the final part, "Sevastopol in August", the narrator describes the siege of Sevastopol and the eventual defeat and withdrawal of the Russian forces.

Passages from "The Sebastopol Sketches"

"The sounds of the firing, growing louder and louder, merged into a continuous rolling thunder."

"The wind bore across the rapid patter of rifle and muskctry fire, a sound like that of rain beating on the windowpane. The black strips were moving through the smoke, drawing nearer and nearer. The sounds of the firing, growing louder and louder, merged into a continuous rolling thunder. The puffs of smoke, which were rising more and more frequently, soon spread along the lines and at last fused into a single, liac-coloured, smoking and developing cloud in which flashes of light and black dots briefly appeared here and there. Then, finally, all the sounds united into one earth-shattering detonation."

"A light breeze was barely rustling the withered leaves....."

"The sun was shining high and brilliant above the bay, which glittered warmly and cheerfully, studded with motionless ships and moving sailboats and skiffs. A light breeze was barely rustling the withered leaves of the scrub oaks near the Telegraph, filling the sails of the small boats and raising a gentle swell."

".... see only this superficial aspect of the man..."

"... as discipline is founded, as often happens in society, on casual fortune or the money principle, it unfailingly ends up either as overweening arrogance on the one hand, or concealed envy and irritation on the other - instead of acting beneficially to unite a mass of men into a single unit, it produces quite the opposite effect. The man who feels unable to inspire respect by virtue of his own intrinsic merits is instinctively afraid of contact with his subordinates and attempts to ward off criticism by means of superficial mannerisms. His subordinates…see only this superficial aspect of the man…"

"… once again the engines of death and
suffering will start their whistling;.."

"Yes, white flags have been raised on the bastion and all along the trench, the flowering valley is filled with stinking corpses, the resplendent sun is descending towards the dark blue sea, and the sea's blue swell is gleaming in the sun's golden rays. Thousands of men are crowding together, studying one another, speaking to one another, smiling at one another. It might be supposed that when these men - Christians, recognizing the same great law of love - see what they have done, they will instantly fall to their knees in order to repent before Him who, when He gave them life, placed in the soul of each, together with the fear of death, a love of the good and the beautiful, and that they will embrace one another with tears of joy and happiness, like brothers. Not a bit of it! The scraps of white cloth will be put away - and once again the engines of death and suffering will start their whistling; once again the blood of the innocent will flow and the air will be filled with their groans and cursing."

∽

"Resurrection"

A wealthy aristocrat is prepared to take extraordinary measures to fix the evil he did to a young woman who has became a prostitute as a result of his seducing her when she was a young serf on his family's estate. The story addresses the life of Russian aristocrats - the fake importance they assign to their roles in society- and the evils that come from the rich, who use "the people" for their own good, while the majority of the population starves and lives in poverty.

Passages from "Resurrection"

"… they were forced outside all the conditions required for a normal and moral human existence ."

"What he had seen during the past three months had left him with the impression that from the whole population living in freedom the government in conjunction with the courts picked out the most highly strung, mettlesome and excitable individuals, the most gifted and the strongest - but less crafty and cautious than other people - and these, who were not one whit more guilty or more dangerous to society than those who were left at liberty, were locked up in goals, halting-stations, hard-labour camps, where they were confined for months and years in utter idleness, material security, and exile from nature, from their families and from useful work. In other words, they were forced outside all the conditions required for a normal and moral human existence ."

"Nekhlyudov undressed, spread his rug on the oilcloth sofa, arranged his leather pillow and lay down, thinking…"

"The clean guest-room smelled of wormwood and sweat, and someone with mighty lungs was rhythmically snoring and making sucking noises behind a partition. A red lamp was burning in front of the ikons. Nekhlyudov undressed, spread his rug on the oilcloth sofa, arranged his leather pillow and lay down, thinking over all he had heard and seen that day. The most terrible spectacle of all for him had been the small boy sleeping in the liquid that oozed from the stinking tub, his head resting on the convict's leg."

"... power to satisfy, for not to satisfy, their desires, and this made her an important and necessary person."

"According to her philosophy the highest good for all men without exception - old and young, schoolboys and generals, educated and uneducated - consisted in sexual intercourse with attractive women, and therefore all men, though they pretended to be occupied with other things, in reality cared for nothing else. She, now, was an attractive woman who had it in her power to satisfy, for not to satisfy, their desires, and this made her an important and necessary person. All her past and present life confirmed the truth of this attitude."

"Nekhlyudov was the only one not to experience this feeling: he was overwhelmed with horror..."

"Thus the secretary ended his reading of the lengthy act of indictment and, having collected up his documents, he resumed his seat, smoothing his long hair with both hands. Everyone drew a sigh of relief in the pleasant knowledge that now the trial had begun, and everything would be made clear and justice be satisfied. Nekhlyudov was the only one not to experience this feeling: he was overwhelmed with horror at the thought of what Maslova, the innocent charming girl he had known ten years ago, might have done."

❧

"My Dream"

The story is about of a fractured relationship between a father and his daughter. The father vows to never have a relationship with his daughter, who leaves the family home and has a child out of wedlock. The father, who is a member of the nobility, refuses to forgive his daughter. Although experiencing poverty the daughter is determined to raise her child alone. Eventually, the father and daughter reconcile after the father comes to terms with his selfish pride

Passages from "My Dream"

"… the horror of it, the horror of it."

"As a daughter she no longer exists for me. Can't you understand? She simply doesn't exist. Still, I cannot possibly leave her to the charity of strangers. I will arrange things so that she can live as she please, but I do not wish to hear of her. Who would ever have thought… the horror of it, the horror of it."

"… the perfect love of a woman for a man, held the promise of life for her."

"Her weakness was the greater, because she had nothing to support her in the struggle. She was weary of society life and she had no affection for her mother. Her father, so she thought, had cast her away from him, and she longed passionately to live and to have done with play. Love, the perfect love of a woman for a man, held the promise of life for her. Her strong, passionate nature, too, was dragging her thither. In the tall, strong figure of this man, with his fair hair and light upturned mustache, under which shone a smile attractive and compelling, she saw the promise of the life for which she longed."

"… but there was no comfort in prayer,.."

"Then her life within began. It was real life, and despite the torture of it, had the possibility been given her, she would not have turned back from it. She began to pray, but there was no comfort in prayer, and her suffering was less for herself than for her father, whose grief she foresaw and understood."

"… he had nothing to forgive, but that he himself needed forgiveness."

"In his pity for her he understood himself. And when he saw himself as he was, he realised how he had wronged her, how guilty he had been in his pride, in his coldness, even in his anger towards her. He was glad that it was he who was guilty, and that he had nothing to forgive, but that he himself needed forgiveness. She took him to her tiny room, and told him how she lived; but she did not show him the child, nor did she mention the past, knowing how painful it would be for him."

∽

"Master and Men"

This story is about a merchant who has this immediate opportunity to purchase a grove at a bargain price, and goes off to complete the deal before someone else takes it. Faced with impending bad weather, he brings along his servant. It's winter and he misjudges the weather, and they are caught in a blizzard, and it becomes a question of survival. The merchant finds himself faced with a test of "selfishness" or "selflessness."

Passages from "Master and Men"

"… he was now really passing from this life of which he was weary…"

"Before he died he asked his wife's forgiveness and forgave her for the cooper. He also took leave of his son and grandchildren, and died sincerely glad that he was relieving his son and daughter-in-law of the burden of having to feed him, and that he was now really passing from this life of which he was weary into that other life which every year and every hour grew clearer and more desirable to him. Whether he is better or worse off there where he woke after his death, whether he was disappointed or found there what he expected, we shall all soon learn."

"… his dead head pressed against his frozen throat:.."

"The snow had hidden the sledge, but the shafts and the kerchief tied to them were still visible. Mukhorty, buried up to his belly in the snow, with the breeching and drugget hanging down, stood all white, his dead head pressed against his frozen throat: icicles hung from his nostrils, his eyes were covered with hoarfrost as though filled with tears, and he had grown so thin in that one night that he was nothing but skin and bone."

"… the horse suddenly planted his forelegs above the height of the sledge, drew up his hind legs also,.."

"… beside the black thing they had noticed, dry, oblong willow-leaves were fluttering, and so he knew it was not a forest but a settlement, but he did not wish to say so. And in fact they had not gone twenty-five yards beyond the ditch before something in front of them, evidently trees, showed up black, and they heard a new and melancholy sound. Nikita had guessed right; it was not a wood, but a row of tall willows with a few leaves still fluttering on them here and there. They had evidently been planted along the ditch round a threshing-floor. Coming up to the willows, which moaned sadly in the wind, the horse suddenly planted his forelegs above the height of the sledge, drew up his hind legs also, pulling the sledge onto higher ground, and turned to the left, no longer sinking up to his knees in snow. They were back on the road."

"... tracks left by the sledge-runners were immediately covered by snow.."

"As soon as they had passed the blacksmith's hut, the last in the village, they realized that the wind was much stronger than they had thought. The road could hardly be seen. The tracks left by the sledge-runners were immediately covered by snow and the road was only distinguished by the fact that it was higher than the rest of the ground. There was a swirl of snow over the fields and the line where sky and earth met could not be seen. The Telyatin forest, usually clearly visible, now only loomed up occasionally and dimly through the driving snowy dust."

❧

"The Wood-Cutting Expedition"

A young Russian soldier, assigned to the Caucasus where he hopes to earn rewards, honor, and a promotion, describes the events he and his fellow soldiers experienced when they came under attack while clearing a way through the forest.

Passages from "The Wood-Cutting Expedition"

"... amid the general silence the melancholy notes of Antonof's song rang out."

"From above the same wretched drizzle was falling; in the atmosphere was the same odour of dampness and smoke; around us could be seen the same bright dots of the dying fires, and amid the general silence the melancholy notes of Antonof's song rang out. And when this ceased for a moment, the faint nocturnal sounds of the camp, the snoring, the clank of a sentinel's musket, and quiet conversation, chimed with it."

"... his glance had a quick and feeble expression; but in his eyes..."

"The wounded man lay on the wagon bottom, holding the sides with both hands. His healthy, broad face had in a few seconds entirely changed; he had, as it were, grown gaunt, and older by several years. His lips were pinched and white, and tightly compressed, with evident effort at self-control; his glance had a quick and feeble expression; but in his eyes was a peculiarly clear and tranquil gleam, and on his blood-stained forehead and nose already lay the seal of death."

"The atmosphere was brisk with the morning frost and the warmth of the spring sun."

"The fog was now completely lifted, and taking the form of clouds, was disappearing slowly in the dark-blue vault of heaven. The unclouded orb of the sun shone bright, and threw its cheerful rays on the steel of the bayonets, the brass of the cannon, on the thawing ground, and the glittering points of the icicles. The atmosphere was brisk with the morning frost

DONALD E. BROWN

and the warmth of the spring sun. Thousands of different shades and tints mingled in the dry leaves of the forest; and on the hard, shining level of the road could be seen the regular tracks of wheel-tires and horse-shoes."

"... strange forms swept through the white folds of the mist."

"The bright disk of the sun, gleaming through the milk-white mist, had now got well up; the purple-grey horizon gradually widened: but, though the view became more extended, still it was sharply defined by the delusive white wall of the fog. In front of us, on the other side of the forest, could be seen a good-sized field. Over the field there spread from all sides the smoke, here black, here milk-white, here purple; and strange forms swept through the white folds of the mist. Far in the distance, from time to time, groups of mounted Tatars showed themselves and occasionally reports from our rifles, guns, and cannon were heard."

✧

THE END

Printed in the United States
by Baker & Taylor Publisher Services